Please remember that this is a library book,
and that it belongs only temporarily to each
person who uses it. Be considerate. Do
not write in this, or any, library book.

Puerto Rico
Ally for Progress

by EARL PARKER HANSON

Consultant to the Department of State
Commonwealth of Puerto Rico

———————

A SEARCHLIGHT ORIGINAL
under the general editorship of

GEORGE W. HOFFMAN   G. ETZEL PEARCY
University of Texas   *United States*
Department of State

———————

D. VAN NOSTRAND COMPANY, INC.
PRINCETON, NEW JERSEY

TORONTO   LONDON

NEW YORK

For Stefansson

Who first taught me that there
is only one geography: the
problems of people, studied in
terms of regionalism.

D. VAN NOSTRAND COMPANY, INC.
120 Alexander St., Princeton, New Jersey
(*Principal Office*)
24 West 40 Street, New York 18, New York

D. Van Nostrand Company, Ltd.
358, Kensington High Street, London, W.14, England

D. Van Nostrand Company (Canada), Ltd.
25 Hollinger Road, Toronto 16, Canada

Published simultaneously in Canada by
D. Van Nostrand Company (Canada), Ltd.

PRINTED IN THE UNITED STATES OF AMERICA

Preface

An intellectual in one of the newly emerging African nations wrote me recently about a problem that worried him. He could see no way in which his country could effectively improve its standards of living without borrowing heavily from the socialism which is so often anathema to the democratic West. I replied that the Puerto Rican experience shows the main problem to be not that of adhering strictly to this or that doctrinaire ideological pattern. The task in hand is to keep the job's *twin* goals—that of raising standards of living and that of strengthening democracy—always in mind and unseparated. Personally, I wrote him, I was convinced that a poor country, emerging from colonialism, could not attain these goals *without* borrowing many things from socialism and even communism, always excepting the sacrifice of human freedom. I pointed out that when Puerto Rico's leader, Luis Muñoz Marín, was once accused of being a dangerous Red, he answered with what might well be adopted as a slogan by the many societies which are throwing off their colonialism while striving not to err into communism's camp. "We are neither radical nor conservative," he said. "We are merely realistic."

In this age of ubiquitous, revolutionary change, we scholars and workers in all the social sciences, from sociology through ethnology and economics to history and geography, could profit from Muñoz's slogan. When doctrinaire orthodoxy fails increasingly to fulfill its task, that of serving human needs, its basic premises must perforce be re-examined and reshaped to meet realism's demands. "Science," my eminent economist friend Herbert Dorn used to say, "must come closer to life and life must come closer to science." The difficult task of the modern Western world—never to permit, in today's revolution, democracy to be sacrificed to the material improvement

3

of life—means that all the social sciences must now draw together and integrate as never before. It also means that we must impart to our students the concept that in this historic era, which is characterized outstandingly by change, our various social disciplines must keep pace, must become as fluid as the social life which they are designed to clarify and serve, must delve deeply into the mechanics of change.

The social sciences, too, have entered an "age of discovery" which calls for much probing and observation in human laboratories. While virtually any society will serve for that purpose, some are better than others, and I particularly recommend Puerto Rico. It is small enough and close enough to the United States to be studied with convenience; its revolution dates back to 1940 and has never abandoned the task of strengthening democracy; the Puerto Rican revolution has by now generated its own ideology which is often unorthodox, but always important.

Since 1952, when the University of Delaware took the first pioneering step, several United States institutions of higher learning, notably Sarah Lawrence College, have periodically sent groups of students to Puerto Rico to study that fluid society itself rather than the several assorted distillates of human experience which we call the social sciences. The results have in every case been remarkable. Faced with the imminent and immense task of taking their individual places in a fast-changing world, the students were almost invariably, and often greatly, stimulated by their study of a fast-changing society. The practice of using Puerto Rico as a laboratory and sending students there is to be highly recommended, and I assure my colleagues in the social sciences that as long as I remain associated with the Puerto Rican government I will do all in my power to further that practice.

EARL PARKER HANSON

San Juan, Puerto Rico
October 10, 1962

Contents

5

List of Maps

I   *Alliance for Progress*

THE easternmost of the Greater Antilles, Puerto Rico is a relatively small tropical island, densely crowded, poor in natural resources, dramatically beautiful, which has in recent years attracted world attention. Since 1951 it has been visited by a steady stream of observers, technicians, distinguished men and women from Latin America, Asia, Africa, Oceania, and Europe, from virtually all of the world's non-communist countries. Today they number more than a thousand a year, and the number is growing. Most of them come from "emerging" societies, from new nations which have shaken off their former colonial status or from old ones which are experiencing the modern world revolution and have set out to expand their economies and reshape their societies. They go to Puerto Rico because, since 1940, the island has managed, accelerated, and guided its own revolution to improve standards of living and strengthen democracy. They want to see how it is that a small and poor society has been able to achieve so much in so short a time. In Puerto Rico's lamentable recent past, admirable present, and possibly glowing future, many of the visitors recognize counterparts of their own national problems and aspirations.

REVOLUTION IN LATIN AMERICA

After growing steadily throughout the past decade, Puerto Rico's importance in the moral and philosophical sense shot up immeasurably on March 13, 1961. That was the day when President Kennedy set a new milestone in the course of inter-American affairs by making his historic "Alliance for Progress" proposal. He said that Latin America is in a state of revolution, that its people—their numbers growing at an alarming rate—now demand something better than their traditional lot of abject poverty coupled with a denial of human freedom. He announced that the United States is eager to enter into a continent-wide alliance to carry out a ten-year crash program to meet those demands. Events in Castro's Cuba undoubtedly influenced the President in his decision to frame so epoch-making a policy, but it is also true that requests and proposals for something resembling the Alliance for Progress have frequently come out of Latin America in recent decades. Three outstanding Latin American leaders, President Rómulo Betancourt of Venezuela, Dr. José Figueres, former President of Costa Rica, and Governor Luis Muñoz Marín of Puerto Rico have done much to shape the President's thinking.

PUERTO RICO'S IMPORTANCE

Three years before Kennedy's announcement, on March 10, 1958, Governor Muñoz Marín had, on invitation, appeared before the Foreign Relations Committee of the United States Senate to give his views on desirable United States policies toward and within the Americas. On that occasion, though without using the words, he also pointed out that Latin America is in the throes of a revolutionary struggle to abolish extreme poverty and strengthen human freedoms. Comparison of Muñoz' statement with Kennedy's leaves little doubt that the two statements are related. In addressing the Senate, the Governor of Puerto Rico urged a United States policy which closely resembled that adopted in 1961. Kennedy, moreover, has shown an acute awareness of Puerto Rico, what it means, and what it has to offer today's strifetorn world. Even before announcing his "alliance" policy, he had stated publicly that Puerto Rico would play an important role in his conduct of inter-American affairs. He sent high officials in his government to San Juan to confer with the governor. Two Puerto Ricans, Dr. Arturo Morales Carrión and Mr. Teodoro Moscoso, were appointed to important posts in the federal government. Dr. Morales had previously been Puerto Rico's Undersecretary of State and now became Deputy Assistant Secretary of State for Latin America. Mr. Moscoso, who had served for nearly two decades in the promotion of his island's outstanding economic growth, left his post as Administrator of the

Puerto Rican Economic Development Administration to become United States ambassador to Venezuela. After a few months in that post he was placed in charge of the entire "Alliance for Progress" program.

There have been some protests against such use of Puerto Rico and Puerto Ricans, emanating largely from left-wing circles which strive stubbornly to maintain the fiction that the island is still a stricken colony of the United States and its leaders are mere venal lackeys of the Yanqui Imperialists. Such objectors insist that the Kennedy proposal is merely a new ruse by which the evil Dollar Diplomats are attempting to transform all the Latin American nations into carbon copies of an unhappy, exploited Puerto Rico. Even in non-communist circles the old, classic Latin American idea that national independence and human freedom are synonymous hangs on tenaciously. In the face of all arguments for the free use of self-determination, it leads a number of uninformed Latin Americans to conclude that Puerto Rico, not being a sovereign republic, *must* be an unhappy, exploited colony. Diametrically opposite views, however, have begun to spread—though perhaps too slowly—throughout Latin America. As for transforming the Latin republics into carbon copies of Puerto Rico, both Muñoz and Kennedy implied in their statements that this would be impossible, that Puerto Rico's "Operation Bootstrap" cannot be duplicated, that no nation can be transformed into an image of another. They specifically spoke against the advisability of even seeming to attempt such a thing.

BILATERAL ACTION

In his discourse of 1958, Muñoz had described his island's modern political economic and social progress in terms which made it clear that he ascribed that progress to a happy collaboration between Puerto Rico and its former imperial master, the United States. The import of his discourse was that since 1941 the United States had already had an alliance for progress with one Latin American society, that such collaboration to accelerate the modern revolution and guide it along democratic lines had been astonishingly successful, and that the underlying idea might well be applied to inter-American affairs. He had stressed the principle of self-determination which had worked so well in Puerto Rico's case, and warned that "it is of paramount importance that the United States or the developed Western powers avoid seeming to ram a doctrine down the throats of those who wish to receive their aid."

Three years later, when announcing his country's willingness to grant such aid, Kennedy said: ". . . If our alliance is to succeed, each Latin nation must formulate long-range plans for its own development. . . ." Each nation differs from all others, geographically, culturally, politically, in the character and aspirations of its people; no one formula-for-salvation can be applied to all of them except the broad one announced by Kennedy, "progress, yes; tyranny, no!"

GEOGRAPHY AND DESTINY

Two important geographic facts, taken together, differentiate Puerto Rico from all other Latin American countries and have played massive roles in shaping the island's history and destiny. They are: 1) Puerto Rico's strategic location at the approaches to the Caribbean Sea and the Isthmus of Panama (See Map 1); and, 2) its relatively small size and truly dramatic paucity of natural resources.When one looks back on Puerto Rico's history, it is as if the island's people had for centuries been saying to themselves: "Our strategic location means that we will always be coveted and ruled by some military power. It dooms us to remain colonial subjects and so deprives us of the freedom and power to help ourselves out of our dreadful poverty. However, even if we had that freedom and power, we would not be able to do much with them; our lack of natural resources dooms us to poverty in any event."

MECHANICS OF COLONIALISM

At the end of the nineteenth century, when the United States took over Puerto Rico as a result of the Treaty of Paris which ended the Spanish-American War, it found an ill, poverty-stricken society which was remarkably unified in the cultural sense as a re-

MAP I

AIR ROUTE DISTANCES FROM PUERTO RICO

TO	VIA	MILES
LONDON	BERMUDA	4400
MADRID	BERMUDA	4000
RIO DE JANEIRO	CARACAS	3200
MEXICO CITY	MIAMI	2250
MIAMI	*direct*	1050
CHICAGO	*direct*	2200
NEW YORK	*direct*	1600

ORIENTATION OF PUERTO RICO

sult of nearly four centuries of oppression by Spain. Officially, in part because the United States wanted to continue being regarded as a non-imperial nation, the island came to be called an "unincorporated territory," as opposed to "incorporated" territories which were destined eventually to become federated states of the Union. Actually it became a colony of the United States with far less freedom to manage its own affairs than it had finally won from Spain at the end of the nineteenth century. There can be no doubt that the United States, its government and people, had the best of intentions toward the newly acquired possession. The fact that the relationship proved not always to be happy can be ascribed in part to cultural differences and in part to the total lack of experience in the management of colonial affairs which the United States brought to the task of governing Puerto Rico.

Throughout the first four decades under the United States, Puerto Rico seemed often to grope in darkness and uncertainty. Again and again, as good North American governors, appointed by the President, were succeeded by bad ones, high hopes and great expectations gave way to despair. Truly, the Puerto Ricans seemed to lack the freedom and powers through which they could help themselves out of abysmal poverty; they were beggars at Uncle Sam's doorstep. On paper they had a certain amount of self-government. After 1900 they could elect their own one-chamber legislature, which was enlarged to two chambers in 1917. They could debate and pass their own measures for the operation of their internal affairs, but that ability was nullified by the governor's power to veto bills passed by the insular law-making body. Through the use of such veto, and through the judicious distribution of patronage, he could destroy any local political party. Since, as Muñoz Marín once wrote, parties don't like to be destroyed, they tended to behave themselves. A colonial politician's first duty after being elected was to remain *persona grata* with the government in Washington; when he didn't he ceased being an active politician. Under those conditions, Puerto Rico's affairs were actually run in Washington; the policies guiding such management were formulated in Washington; almost any minor federal official who had anything to do with Puerto Rican affairs often had more power than did a Puerto Rican cabinet member. It was a familiar political pattern (now abolished), which is recognized by virtually all visitors from recent colonies in Asia and Africa.

ABSENTEE ECONOMIC AND POLITICAL DOMINATION

Long before the Spanish-American War, the Puerto Ricans had clamored at Washington's door for free trade, for the duty-free entry into the United States of such exports as sugar. Now, at last, after coming under the United States flag, they were granted such free trade. But now, too, corporate United States capital followed the flag and established itself in Puerto Rico—particularly in the sugar industry. Despite a federal law under which no corporation was permitted to own or control more than five hundred acres of Puerto Rican land, four powerful sugar companies acquired estates rang- ing in size up to nearly 55,000 acres—only half of which were usu- ally planted to sugar while the rest were held in reserve. Those four came to exercise enormous political power, in part because they were "American" interests, in part because they could control the votes in elections. The many thousands of men who worked for them voted as they were told, lest they lose their miserable starva- tion wages; the thousands of the voting poor who didn't depend for their living on the sugar companies were given small bribes— up to two dollars—for voting "correctly." By such means the com- panies made sure that the legislature was filled largely by sugar- lawyers who were careful to do nothing as law-makers which they would later come to regret as lawyers serving the sugar interests.

On paper, Puerto Rico's economy improved dramatically, year by year. The island's external trade grew by leaps and bounds, and ex- ports usually exceeded imports by some $10 million, leaving a favor- able balance of trade. Writing as a journalist in New York, how- ever, Muñoz Marín compared the trade-balance with that of a bur- glarized house, in which exports also exceed imports. When one considered the balance of payments—high profits exported by the absentee sugar companies, high freight rates paid for shipping be- tween Puerto Rico and the mainland United States, rents paid on absentee-owned properties—, one found, as Bailey and Justine Diffie did in their memorable study *Porto Rico, A Broken Pledge,* that Puerto Rico was annually exporting something like $20 million in order to maintain an economy which brought in only half of that amount.

To some extent throughout the Spanish days, but increasingly under the United States, Puerto Rico lived under the classic feudal- ism which the *conquistadores* had once imported bodily from medieval Europe, with a "one-crop" economy supporting a two- class society in which the small upper class held all the power while the large masses lived lives of misery, void of human freedoms. In

1929, Muñoz, then a poet and free-lance journalist, wrote as follows about his native island: "By now the development of large, absentee-owned sugar estates, the rapid curtailment in the planting of coffee . . . and the concentration of cigar manufacture in the hands of the American trust, have combined to make it a land of beggars and millionaires, of flattering statistics and distressing realities. More and more it becomes a factory worked by peons, fought over by lawyers, bossed by absentee industrialists, and clerked by politicians. It is now Uncle Sam's second largest sweatshop."

POPULATION PRESSURES

At the turn of the century, Puerto Rico's population was less than one million. By 1940 it had climbed to 1,869,000 and five years later it surpassed two million. The island's birth rate, though now declining, has long been regarded by demographers as one of the world's most explosive, its density of population one of the world's highest. Until the crash year, 1929, new capital investments, though largely by absentees, tended to keep the economy expanding, though never rapidly enough to keep pace with the growth of population. After 1929, however, the economy contracted, while the population which it was designed to support soared alarmingly. Capital investments ceased; the sale of sugar to the United States came to be regulated by a quota, its amounts curtailed drastically; the sugar planters were paid bonuses for the cane which they refrained from growing; the thousands of cane cutters who were thrown out of work by the quota system were sustained, poorly, by federal relief.

THE WORLD DEPRESSION

The United States undertook to spend millions of dollars for relief of various kinds, simply to keep too many people from dying of starvation on the streets, the plazas, and the country lanes. In 1935, relief gave way to "reconstruction," through which, in a spirit of enlightened imperialism, efforts were made to reshape the island's economy in such a manner as to function better than formerly for the benefit of the island's people. Both the relief and the reconstruction were widely hailed as indications and results of North American generosity, but they proved to be too little and too late. Officials in Washington were only vaguely aware that the very institution of colonialism was breaking down in Puerto Rico, as it was in the world's other colonies. At the same time, a new political status for colonialism's effective replacement had not yet been invented.

Illness and despair, hunger, lethargy, and death were the order of those unhappy days. The desire for Puerto Rico's independence spread far and wide. The Nationalists, who in 1932 had ceased being a party because they failed to poll sufficient votes in that year's election to retain party status, now took guns and began to assassinate Americans. The bitter vendetta which arose between the Nationalists and the police took a number of lives and stirred passions to fever heat. Washington officials mistakenly equated a desire for independence with hatred of the United States and dangerous terroristic leanings. Their repressive actions and dangerous political maneuverings for a time virtually scuttled United States prestige on the island.

A brilliant young senator belonging to the Liberal Party, a warm friend of the United States, advocated Puerto Rico's independence "as a matter of mutual convenience to the American taxpayers and the people of Puerto Rico." His name was Luis Muñoz Marín, and he was absolutely, completely, and openly against the use of violence for the achievement of his island's political sovereignty. The son of Puerto Rico's most honored political leader, Luis Muñoz Rivera, he was also a brilliant leader, thinker, and speaker in his own right, enormously popular among the barefoot poor, the so-called "jíbaros" in the mountainous interior. For such reasons and others, Washington's top officialdom began to regard him as an enemy, thereby embarrassing the Liberal Party's leaders. In 1937, undoubtedly with a nudge from Washington, Muñoz Marín was expelled from the Liberal Party. It seemed obvious at the time that his star had set, that he had been politically destroyed. No other party could afford to take in a man who was *persona non grata* in Washington. Cynicism bordering on despair seized the intellectuals who had, together with the *jíbaros,* constituted his following. A number of

them migrated to the mainland United States; others went underground in the sense of thereafter keeping quiet about American
policies and actions, lest somebody report them to federal officials as
dangerous subversives. The tensions were explosive; the psychological explosion was not long in coming.

REVOLUTION

Rejected by his party, penniless, Muñoz Marín gathered his remaining friends and followers about him and organized a new
political entity, the Popular Democratic Party, whose slogan was
"Bread, Land and Liberty." Working feverishly, the little band se-
cured enough petition signatures to permit it to go to the 1940 election. The campaign for that election began in 1938, with speech
after speech, in one town and hamlet after another, again and again
in each, with a revolutionary message designed primarily to lift
the Puerto Rican people out of their lethargy, to give them hope
and above all faith in themselves. In effect, Muñoz dealt with his
island's geographic realities as follows: "It is true that we lack the
political power to help ourselves; it is true that even if we had that
power, we would still lack natural resources with which to improve
our lives. But it is also true that *we have never in our history, con-
sciously and with determination, set out to do the very best we can
with the powers and resources we do have. Let us try that and see
what happens."*

In his campaign he hammered away at the evils of selling votes, at
the dignity and power of a man's vote, the need for respecting it
and using it in good conscience. As a result of that and subsequent
campaigns the practice of selling votes, once virtually a Puerto
Rican culture trait, has now been long abolished.

POLITICAL STATUS AND SOCIAL IMPROVEMENT

He told people that Puerto Rico's political status was not an issue in that campaign. "I have long and openly been for independence, but I am not now campaigning for that or any other political
status. What I *am* campaigning for is the improvement in your lives
and those of your children which you *must* desire regardless of

whether you want Puerto Rico to become a republic, a state of the North American Union, or anything else." His campaign promises comprised, exclusively, such matters as industrialization, reforms in agriculture and land tenure, rural electrification, social legislation, improved and expanded education and public health facilities. The poor loved his speeches; the rich and sophisticated, who had previously regarded him as a dangerous radical, laughed at them. They maintained that, even if by some terrible mischance he *should* manage to win the election, he lacked the power to deliver on his promises. The power was held by Washington, where Muñoz was *persona non grata*.

The 1940 campaign was truly revolutionary in the sense that Muñoz threatened to wrest power from the ruling capital when he promised his people a number of things which he, as a colonial subject, could not deliver. The question of whether it constituted a revolution against the United States or against the institution of exploitative colonialism, with its evils of poverty and lack of freedom, remained to be settled by Washington's reaction to it. He won the election by a bare margin, becoming President of the Puerto Rican Senate and the island's undisputed political leader. There was much consternation in Washington, but President Roosevelt preceded Kennedy by twenty years in recognizing the revolution's aims and offering to abet them. Apprised of Muñoz' victory and startling aims, he wrote the latter a warm letter, praising those aims highly and offering the federal government's full cooperation toward achieving them.

THE END OF COLONIALISM

That letter from Roosevelt marked the actual end of Puerto Rico's colonialism. For when a colonial subject wins an election on a revolutionary platform, and the ruling nation then says "it is a fine idea, we will help you all we can," the *spirit* of colonialism has fled. From then on, the abolition of its forms is only a matter of time, of step-by-step evolution. Today Puerto Rico is no longer a colony. As a "Free, Associated State," it is entirely self-governing in the management of its internal affairs, and closely associated with the

United States through its own choice, expressed through the processes of self-determination.

Today Puerto Rico's most important resource, beside the Puerto Ricans themselves, is its excellent relationship with the United States, including its proximity to the United States, the political system it has worked out jointly with the United States, its position within the American tariff wall, its access to American capital and markets, and its financial position, under which it enjoys federal bounty on a basis of equality with the fifty states without contributing to the federal treasury.

After the 1940 election, a short-sighted or vindictive federal government could have sent a governor to Puerto Rico to ruin Muñoz and his party by merely vetoing their new bills as fast as they passed them. Instead, Roosevelt sent Dr. Rexford Tugwell, an embattled, crusading reformer, to collaborate with Muñoz on the mammoth task of creating a new Puerto Rico.

TRANSFORMATION

The revolution got under way with unprecedented energy virtually the day the Popular Democratic Party took over the government. Machinery was set up, not only for enforcing the Five-Hundred-Acre law by expropriating lands held by the absentee corporations in excess of the legal limit, but also for their adequate use and distribution after the government had acquired them. A government Industrial Development Company, patterned after Chile's and consisting at first of two men and a typewriter, was created and told to go to work on the task of industrialization. Public health measures were pushed with vigor, and studies of the island's educational problems begun. In the latter field, the new government could for a time do little, since the Commissioner of Education was still appointed by the President with consent of the Senate and was responsible to the Congress for his educational policies. But that situation meant merely that appropriate planning was called for to devise political action through which Puerto Rico could eventually, as it did in 1948, get its own educational policies firmly within its own hands.

The men who had taken control of the government were in essence poets, dreamers with great visions, who lacked practical experience in governmental affairs. Mistakes were made, recognized, and corrected. False starts were pulled up short and replaced by fresh starts. There was occasional friction between Governor Tugwell and the Puerto Rican leaders, but on the whole they worked well and effectively together. The island's ultra-conservatives, the powerful large land-owners, screamed socialism and worse, sent commissions to Washington to protest against such un-American activities, attacked the new government incessantly in the conservative press, but got nowhere. World War II hampered the task of transformation in many ways, but there was no relenting. The effort was intensified daily; the hopes of the people and their faith in themselves as Puerto Ricans began to soar. Muñoz came to see those released and mounting hopes as among the most powerful forces working on his side. In 1961 he was to say that the most important result of the Alliance for Progress would have to be in the psychological field, in arousing the hopes of Latin America's stricken millions, and so also their faith in the new policies.

ACHIEVEMENTS

Since the election of 1940, and with the help and support of the United States, Puerto Rico has, among other things:

(1) Greatly expanded its power network and launched a remarkable program of industrialization to give employment and to strengthen and diversify the economy;

(2) Made strong headway in the diversification, modernization, and augmented production of its agricultural plant;

(3) Virtually trebled its per capita annual income in terms of purchasing power and improved the distribution of that income;

(4) Created one of the hemisphere's most effective public health services and reduced its death rate to a figure lower than that of the continental United States;

(5) Greatly expanded its educational system and taken drastic steps toward reshaping it to fit modern needs; reduced illiteracy below that of any other Latin American society;

(6) Extended that great impetus to all classes of Puerto Ricans to the point where thousands are today "civically employed" and giving their thoughts and labors to improving their own lives, instead of expecting their government to do everything for them;

(7) Created social and economic conditions under which its former explosive birth rate has turned the corner and is declining rapidly, thus bringing the society ever nearer the point where population will finally be in balance with the productive effort;

(8) Abolished its former colonial status and created an unprecedented political relationship with its erstwhile imperial rulers which permits the former colony to proceed with its development at an unprecedented pace.

DETERMINISM VERSUS DETERMINATION

The most important lesson taught by that story to political leaders, planners, geographers, and the like is that, while geographic and environmental realities may be immutable, the ways in which such realities can be utilized are not. They vary over an enormous, incalculable range. In 1947, Dr. Robert Platt of Chicago announced the then almost heretical dictum that determinism of *any* kind has no place in geographical thought. While modern Puerto Rico proves him right, it also proves that "determination"—a people's will to make the most of what it has, integrating social, political, and economic action so closely as to defy all efforts on the part of social scientists to pry them apart—has a very definite place in the thinking of all, geographers included, who strive to understand man's life within its geographic setting.

Strategic Location

In May 1493, Pope Alexander VI issued, on successive days, two bulls which were to roil the Western world's political scene for centuries to come. On the third of that month, he gave to the Catholic Kings of Spain and their heirs and successors the countries and islands discovered by their envoys and to be discovered thereafter ":together with all their dominions, cities, camps, places and villages, and all right, jurisdictions and appurtenances of the same." Addressing himself to the Spanish Monarch, he strictly forbade "all persons of no matter what rank, estate, degree, order, or condition to dare without your special permit . . . to go for the sake of trade or any reason whatever, to the said islands and countries after they have been discovered and found by your envoys or persons sent out for that purpose." The following day he went further and in effect divided the entire non-Christian world, known and yet to be discovered, between Spain and Portugal. He drew a line north and south on the Atlantic and assigned to Spain a monopoly on exploration, discovery, and occupation in the immense territories lying west of that line, and to Portugal in those stretching toward the east.

CHALLENGE FROM NORTHWESTERN EUROPE

While those papal edicts were designed in part to make a Spanish lake out of the Caribbean Sea, the basic principle of possession by virtue of discovery was eventually replaced by that of possession by virtue of effective occupation. Spain lacked men and means for occupying and defending all the Caribbean lands, large and small. Northwestern Europe's internal pressures, creating a desperate need to expand geographically as well as economically, were every bit as great as were those of the Iberian nations. England, France, and Holland challenged Pope Alexander's discriminatory bull almost immediately. The sixteenth and seventeenth centuries saw savage fighting in the Caribbean area, as a result of which one island after another, one section of the mainland after another, fell to the three encroaching countries. For instance, Curaçao became Dutch in 1634, Jamaica English in 1655, and Haiti French in 1697.

Situated between the Caribbean and the wide Atlantic, Puerto Rico became a bastion for the attempted exclusion of enemies from Spain's *Mare Clausum,* a sentry box for guarding somebody else's empire. The story of San Juan's massive fortifications has been recorded in an engaging book, *A History of the Harbor Defenses of San Juan, P.R., Under Spain, 1509-1898,* by Lieutenant Edward A. Hoyt, published in 1943 by the Antilles Coast Artillery Command.

Puerto Rico's first settlers, relatively few in number, found the island populated by the rather docile Arawak Indians who were easily enslaved, but soon, because they could not adapt to slavery, had to be replaced by African Negroes. But the Spanish settlers, like the Arawaks before them, were harassed by the fierce, seafaring Caribs who used Puerto Rico as a way-station on their voyages from South America all the way to the Mississippi Delta. The first forts were actually fortified houses in which to safeguard gold and from which to combat the marauding Caribs as well as the occasionally rebelling Arawaks. They began to be built in 1514 under orders from King Ferdinand of Spain, who wanted to be sure that "in case of rebellion our treasure will be secure." Built for the protection of Puerto Rico and its settlers, those structures had no imperial implications.

The first Spanish settlers, arriving in Puerto Rico in 1508 (Santo Domingo had begun to be colonized in 1496, and Cuba's settlement began in 1510), realized quite early that they were premature *conquistadores.* Had they waited a few years before coming to the New World they might have been able to gain, elsewhere, far more wealth and glory than their poor little island offered them. Their production of gold, never very important, declined sharply in 1540 and ceased entirely thirty years later. In 1519, when Cortés conquered Mexico with its fabulous wealth, Puerto Rico's envious settlers felt their full share of the excitement which news of the feat sent through the European world. When news came in 1533 of the conquest of Peru by Pizarro and Almagro, most of them felt swindled and wanted to move to the lush economic gardens which had been wrested from the Incas. Even the most firmly established sighed "may God take me to Peru," but the Spanish authorities could not afford to allow so important a strategic position to be abandoned. They flogged those who were caught trying to leave the island, at times cut off their feet, and eventually threatened the death penalty for any discovered attempt at departure.

THE CONFLICT

The urgent need to fortify San Juan began to be realized and reported to the Spanish kings even before the conquest of Peru. A French corsair had entered the sacred Caribbean Sea in 1505. In 1527 an English vessel appeared in San Juan harbor, apparently on a voyage of reconnaissance with ominous implications. The Caribs invaded the harbor in 1529 and stole a ship, returning the next year to lay waste certain areas adjoining the town. In 1530 San Juan's colonial council sent a desperate message to Emperor Charles V, saying in effect: "Let the port be fortified, or the island will be deserted."

Constructon of the first true fort was begun in 1533 and completed in 1540. This was La Fortaleza, which serves today, after innumerable additions and changes, as the governor's residence, the seat of the executive offices, and a major tourist attraction. Even before it was completed, however, the fort proved to be mislocated and virtually useless from the military point of view.

French pirates increased their pressure on San Juan, and construction of a new fort, El Morro, was begun in 1539. But the work proceeded slowly, while cannon and balls, arquebuses, javelins, protective breast plates and helmets, to say nothing of soldiers to use such things, arrived even more slowly from Spain.

ENGLISH ATTACKS

With the rise of England as an important maritime power, Spain had dramatic incentives for speeding up her Caribbean defenses. Sir Francis Drake became well known in the West Indies through his bold Caribbean raids in 1567, 1570, and 1572. In 1586, after his epic voyage to the Pacific, he returned to sack three of Spain's most vital bases: Cartagena, Santo Domingo, and Saint Augustine. He could not hold them, but was fully expected to return to establish an English foothold from which further to harrass Spain's Caribbean trade and the treasure galleons carrying gold and silver from Mexico and Peru. After Drake and inclement weather had, in 1588, destroyed the great Spanish Armada which had been assembled to destroy English sea-power in English waters, San Juan's fortifications became even more important. They were tested in 1592, when Fort El Morro had its first serious encounter with an enemy. The English captain, Christopher Newport, came to San Juan, skirmished with Spanish forces, chased a Spanish frigate into the harbor, and sailed off with a liberated English ship which had presumably been captured by the Spaniards for engaging in illicit trade with their colonies.

News came in 1595 that Drake, in England, was preparing a major fleet, intending to capture the Isthmus of Panama and so to cut the all-important line between Peru and Spain. The spies reported further that Queen Elizabeth had ordered him to stop at San Juan enroute, and capture a great treasure which had been transferred from a wrecked galleon to the Fortaleza. When Drake arrived on November 22 the defenders were ready for him and drove him off after some days of fierce fighting. He sailed for Panama without the Fortaleza treasure, died of dysentery, and was buried at sea.

In 1598 the Earl of Cumberland arrived with a great fleet, landed troops east of San Juan, and stormed Fort El Morro from its poorly protected land side. The English took San Juan and ruled Puerto Rico for 157 days, but finally they were driven off by an epidemic among their troops.

DUTCH ATTACKS

Feverishly, the returning Spaniards now set to work to mend their damaged defenses. El Morro was improved and strengthened on the land side; several smaller forts were added in various locations. The work was completed by the time war broke out between Holland and Spain in 1625. The Dutch arrived September 25 of that year, with a fleet of 17 ships and possibly a thousand fighting men. They entered the harbor, took the city, and burned much of it, including the Fortaleza. They besieged El Morro, demanded surrender, and threatened annihilation to the valiant governor and his beleaguered troops. But in the end, on November 1, they had to withdraw again, leaving behind several capital ships and some four hundred dead. That occasion, and subsequent Dutch corsair activities in the Caribbean, help to explain the odd fact that the Puerto Ricans, although an island people depending for their lives on seaborne commerce, have never been a seafaring people. They were afraid to venture from their island "lest the Dutchmen catch them."

The lessons taught by the Dutch invaders resulted in more fortifications. During the decades between 1630 and 1650, the city came to be surrounded by a great wall. In 1897, when it was obviously no longer useful, the land side of that wall was torn down, in a burst of patriotic enthusiasm, by San Juan's progress-minded citizens. Their frenetic action is today deplored by equally patriotic Puerto Ricans who are laboring, with much success, house by house and street by street, to restore "Old San Juan" to a semblance of its former appearance.

In 1631 work was begun on another fort, even more massive than El Morro. This new structure was San Cristóbal, designed to guard the city's land approaches. Other smaller forts were added or strengthened.

SAN JUAN, A BASE OF OPERATIONS

A number of naval expeditions were organized in San Juan harbor during the second half of the seventeenth century. They sallied forth, according to Spanish accounts, to combat pirates and smugglers on the Caribbean Sea; the English version was that they were sent out to harass and plunder legitimate British shipping. Puerto Rico was a troublesome neighbor to the British in the Caribbean. When Spain sided against England in the American War of Independence, plans were drafted in London for capturing the island. By now, however, San Juan's military strength was too great, and England's too spread out, to make the venture practical.

Now the English tried horse-trading. Having irritated their Spanish enemies no end in 1704 by taking Gibraltar, they offered, in 1781 and several times thereafter, to swap "The Rock" for Puerto Rico. There was no doubt that Spain wanted Gibraltar, but not that badly. Counter offers made by Madrid—for instance, to substitute Santo Domingo for Puerto Rico in an exchange—were rejected by London; England wanted Puerto Rico or nothing.

THE   END OF AN ERA

Spain declared war on England in 1796, and Sir Ralph Abercromby arrived at San Juan the following year with a mighty fleet of sixty vessels, carrying about six hundred cannon. He besieged and blockaded the city but failed to breach its defenses, finally withdrawing after some two weeks of strenuous but unsuccessful effort. San Juan was now left in peace for an entire century, until the Spanish-American War.

RISE OF THE UNITED STATES

The nineteenth century was marked on the one hand by the breakup of Spain's great American empire, leaving only Puerto Rico and Cuba in Madrid's hands, and on the other by the emergence of the United States as a world power. Near the century's end it was certain that the United States would soon undertake to build the Panama Canal and would therefore need Puerto Rico as a point from which to guard its approaches. Rear Admiral T. Mahan, whose writings on naval strategy and power influenced Theodore Roosevelt as much as they did the German Kaiser, wrote that Puerto Rico was to the projected Panama Canal what Malta was to the Suez Canal. Moreover, the Monroe Doctrine seemed to demand that the United States acquire strong bases in the Caribbean; Spain was too weak to prevent further European encroachments. Finally, the United States had turned from a debtor to a creditor nation and had capital for export which, after the day's fashion, wanted to follow the flag. A struggle between the United States and Spain began to seem inevitable, and the explosion which sank the battleship *Maine* in Havana harbor was merely the shot of a starting pistol.

THE SPANISH-AMERICAN WAR

The war's theaters of operation were Cuba, the Philippines, and Puerto Rico, precisely the three points which were coveted by the United States. Admiral Sampson bombarded San Juan and proved the city's fortifications to be obsolete. One of his shells penetrated an eighteen-foot wall at El Morro and exploded in an interior chamber. But the bombardment was not enough; there seemed to be danger that Spain would capitulate, and so end the war, before the United States had occupied Puerto Rico. Hastily General Miles and his troops were landed on the island's south coast and marched over the mountains to San Juan, hailed by the civilian population as liberators and encountering military resistance only in the form of a few insignificant skirmishes. On December 10, 1898, by the Treaty of Paris, the island was ceded to the United States.

MILITARY IMPORTANCE TO THE UNITED STATES

The new rulers lost no time in converting Puerto Rico into a modern military base, and the monies so expended have long played an important role in the island's economy. The activity was accelerated greatly in the years preceding America's entry into World War I, which also saw our acquisition, by purchase from Denmark and primarily for military reasons, of the Virgin Islands.

The early years of World War II, before Pearl Harbor, saw feverish military preparations in Puerto Rico and other Caribbean areas. The famous deal in which Roosevelt traded fifty over-age destroyers for the right to establish bases on British Caribbean islands pointed up the importance, to the United States, of the entire area with its approaches to Panama. Roosevelt Roads, at Puerto Rico's eastern end, was created as a mammoth naval base during the early years when the war was going badly for England. The main idea was to create a great anchorage, between Puerto Rico proper and Vieques Island, capable of holding the entire British navy in the event of a German victory. Work was even begun on an enormous protecting mole, extending from Vieques and possibly designed to reach to the Puerto Rican mainland. It was stopped, however, after the Japanese demonstrated at Pearl Harbor what can happen to warships sitting like ducks in a sheltered port.

During both World Wars, Puerto Rico's importance to the enemy was shown by the intensive submarine campaign through which Germany blockaded the island and sank scores of ships in an effort to starve it out.

NEW CONCEPTS OF STRATEGIC IMPORTANCE

The entire basic concept of warfare was changed by Germany's rocket bombardment of London and America's atom-bombing of Hiroshima. Year by year, the ensuing intense program of research and development has produced new weapons which steadily decrease the military importance of Puerto Rico's geographic location. From far out in the Atlantic, for instance, surface ships and submarines can now launch deadly rockets at the Panama Canal without ever coming within sight of Puerto Rico. Moreover, there is a growing suspicion throughout the world that today's deadly weapons, by threatening total destruction, have already succeeded in outlawing war itself as the final means for enforcing national policies. The extent to which that suspicion is justified is also the extent to which geographers must now re-examine their former concepts of strategic location, must give them new meanings and new values.

Puerto Rico's diminishing military importance has in recent years resulted in certain diminutions of United States defense expenditures on the island. At the same time the Puerto Ricans themselves busily re-examining many of their former basic premises, have come to realize that a land may be strategically located in senses other than the military, and that such location can be a resource, exploitable economically.

STRATEGIC COMMERCIAL LOCATION

The island's position in relation to tuna fish is one economic resource. Until a few years ago, virtually all the tuna fish canned and consumed in the United States were caught in the waters near the Galapagos Islands, canned on the United States Pacific coast, and then shipped via the long and expensive railroad haul to the Atlantic states which constituted the products' principal markets. But then it was realized that the Galapagos Islands are so much nearer to Puerto Rico than to California that transporting the tuna there was well worth the Panama Canal charges, while ocean transportation from Puerto Rico to the Atlantic States was shorter and considerably less expensive than rail transportation from the Pacific coast. The result was the establishment by private industry of a tuna fish cannery in the port of Ponce in 1953. Subsequently, Puerto Rico's importance as a tuna-fish center was enhanced by the discovery of rich fishing grounds in the South Atlantic. The original plant at the Ponce seaport has been enlarged since 1953, and another plant has in recent years been opened at Mayaguez, at the Island's western end. At the time of the present writing, a third company is ready to build a cannery in Mayaguez.

FREE TRADE ZONE

Puerto Rico's central location between the United States and Latin America is also beginning to be put to better commercial use than it has been hitherto. An international free trade zone is today (1961) being constructed in Mayaguez, into which foreign nations can ship parts and goods duty-free for such operations as assembly and packaging. Italian candies, for instance, might be sent there in bulk without paying duty, packaged, and re-exported to Latin American countries. If they are shipped from the zone to the United States, or into Puerto Rico proper, the duty charged, since American labor was used in the packaging, will be less than that which would have been charged had the candies come packaged from Italy. The same treatment will be accorded to such things as Italian scooters and typewriters, German and French automobiles, and the like, which may be shipped to Mayaguez in parts for assembly in the trade zone. Meanwhile, Puerto Rico's representation in Europe to drum up business has been enlarged and strengthened.

As this book is being written, firms engaged in the manufacture of radios, pipe–fittings, prefabricated houses, fabrics, and agricultural equipment are showing an interest in establishing plants in the zone. Two distinguished visitors from Iceland, who visited Puerto Rico in 1961, grasped the free trade zone's potential importance immediately, and so also Puerto Rico's strategic commercial location. Icelanders today ship a part of their fish-catch, frozen in bulk, to Massachusetts, where they operate a factory to manufacture fishsticks, most of which are shipped by rail to California. However, if they had a factory in Mayaguez, they could probably bring in the frozen fish duty-free, obtain labor at somewhat lower rates than those they have to pay in Massachusetts, and save considerably by shipping the finished product to California by steamer rather than by rail.[1]

STRATEGIC LOCATION, POLITICALLY

No doubt other advantages accruing from the island's location will be discovered and put to work in the years to come, or will develop as the Caribbean's political and commercial scene continues its present kaleidoscopic changes. The Caribbean Commission, which grew out of the over-age-destroyer deal mentioned above, is an example in the political field. Originally created as an organization through which the United States and Great Britain could col-

[1] The scheme is imaginative and indicates the scope of Puerto Rico's developmental planning. But there is some chance that it may prove to have been a false start. Mayaguez' port facilities are small and inadequate for much modern shipping, technically unable to accommodate cargoes packed in trailers or large containers. Moreover, trends in today's ocean shipping are toward the elimination of minor ports. Had the free trade zone been located in Ponce or San Juan, it would undoubtedly have had a far greater chance for success than it does in Mayaguez. Trial and error, however, must inevitably mark the course of every newly developing society.

laborate in the wartime handling of their respective Caribbean affairs, the Commission was enlarged after the war to include France and the Netherlands. It was in effect a special organ of the four Caribbean imperial powers, functioning at a time when colonialism was obsolete and was disappearing rapidly everywhere on earth. Puerto Ricans served a number of years as delegates to the Caribbean Commission, but they represented the United States rather than their own society.

In 1952, Puerto Rico became self-governing as a commonwealth. The region's former British colonies later banded into a self-governing "Caribbean Federation," which was dissolved in 1962. Dutch possessions have also emerged from their former colonial status, and the French islands of Guadalupe and Martinique have been incorporated as departments of metropolitan France. As a result of that movement of liberation, the former, imperial Caribbean Commission has voluntarily disbanded itself, to be succeeded by the present "Caribbean Organization," whose members are the former colonies themselves and over whose actions the United States, Britain, France, and the Netherlands now have no control. The fact that the new organization's headquarters and secretariat are in San Juan attests again to Puerto Rico's mounting importance in international affairs.

MORAL IMPORTANCE

Finally, there is such a thing as strategic location in the moral or cultural sense. As pointed out in Chapter I, Puerto Rico has begun to play an important role in hemispheric affairs, not only because it is centrally located between the United States and South America and is therefore accessible from both sides, but also because, as Latin Americans who have come to terms with Anglo-America, the Puerto Ricans have been pioneers in a trend which must now sweep all the Americas.

The forts which attest to the island's former military importance have now become tourist attractions. The swelling stream of tourists and other visitors is one more manifestation of Puerto Rico's strategic location in the commercial sense.

III   *The Physical Base,*
Resources, and Problems

D<small>EPRESSION</small> conditions of the 1930's gave rise to widespread interest in the systematic appraisal of social and economic problems which is known as "planning." Organized in Puerto Rico first within the federal Relief Administration and later as an activity of the Reconstruction Administration, this planning was done largely by young intellectuals, a number of them faculty members in the university who gave a part of their time to studying their country's ills and working toward solutions. They learned much, but the results of their labors were scant. As a consequence, they tended to be pessimistic about the feasibility of planning in a capitalist society, and especially in a colony of the world's most powerful capitalist nation. However, the Planning Division of the Reconstruction Administration was later, after the Puerto Ricans had begun to take the solution of their problems into their own hands, to prove to have been an invaluable incubator of ideas for action as well as of men and women to carry out, modify, and amplify those ideas.

A number of circumstances contributed to the planners' discouragement during the 1930's, among them the fact that planning, as a federal activity rather than a function of the Puerto Rican government, was too widely separated from possibilities of execution and so became a somewhat sterile intellectual exercise. Also contributing to the planners' discouragement was the fact that the island's government was in the hands of the ultra-conservative large landowners, who resented the New Deal with its promises of progress along brand new lines and who bitterly opposed social and economic changes under which their own feudal powers were threatened.

Finally, the inventories of resources with which to work—the island's physical nature and its all-but-overwhelming poverty in nature's economic gifts—constituted massive deterrents to optimism.

THE PHYSICAL BASE

Roughly rectangular in shape, a hundred miles by thirty-five, Puerto Rico has an area of 3,454 square miles, including the adjacent islands of Vieques and Mona, which are under San Juan's jurisdiction. Only two of the federated states, Rhode Island and Delaware, are smaller than Puerto Rico.

As discussed in Chapter VI, distances from mainland ports, 1600 miles from New York and 1000 from Miami, pose special economic problems. While rates for air travel between Puerto Rico and the continental states are remarkably low, the cost of shipping by American steamers is notoriously the world's highest, a fact which complicates the process of economic development.

TOPOGRAPHY

As shown by Map 2, Puerto Rico consists essentially of a complex of mountains, surrounded by a coastal plain. The mountains, their rocks including Quaternary sediments, Tertiary limestones of all degrees of purity and hardness, Cretacious shales, conglomerates, plutonic intrusives, and old volcanic flows, rise to a maximum height of 4,398 above sea level. However, they comprise the tops of a submarine range. Immediately north of Puerto Rico is Bronson's Deep, more than 27,000 feet below the ocean's surface and one of the world's most profound submarine chasms. Measured from its bottom, to give a total altitude of about 31,500 feet, Puerto Rico's mountains may well be the world's highest.

In his *Geografía de Puerto Rico,* Dr. Rafael Picó states that "approximately 55 per cent of the island's surface lies between sea-level and 500 feet; 21 per cent lies between 500 and 1,000 feet, and 24 per cent above 1,000 feet. Fifty-eight per cent of the lands above 1,000 feet (14 per cent of the island's total), and 49 per cent of those between 500 and 1,000 feet (10 per cent of the island's total), have slopes of 45 degrees and more. In terms of grades, almost one-fourth of the island slopes 45 degrees or more; in terms of altitude, approximately half of the total area lies below 500 feet above sea-level." [Translation by E.P.H.] About 40 per cent of the total area is composed of mountains; 35 per cent is hilly, and only 25 per cent is reasonably level. Less than half of the area lying between sea level and 500 feet is sufficiently level for agriculture.

THE CLIMATE

While Puerto Rico lies within the north tropical zone, just above 18 degrees N. latitude, its climate is modified by the steady trade winds. As elsewhere in the tropics, temperature variations between summer and winter tend to be smaller than those between day and night. The highest temperature ever recorded in San Juan was 96 degrees, which is considerably lower than the peaks in Kansas City

MAP 2

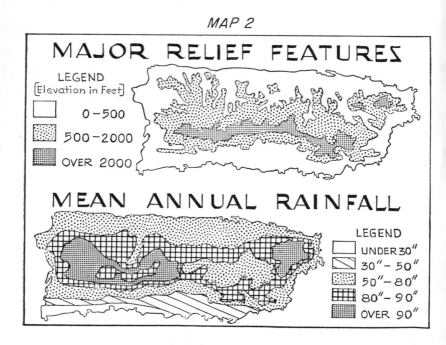

MAJOR RELIEF FEATURES

LEGEND
[Elevation in Feet]

0 – 500
500 – 2000
OVER 2000

MEAN ANNUAL RAINFALL

LEGEND

UNDER 30"
30" – 50"
50" – 80"
80" – 90"
OVER 90"

and Washington, D.C. The mean annual temperature on the coastal plains is 78 degrees. In the interior, at altitudes above 3,000 feet, it is some ten degrees lower.

The interior mountains have a decided influence on the distribution of rainfall. The steady trade winds, blowing in from approximately ENE, are forced to rise when they reach the mountains. Cooled by the rising, they drop most of their moisture on the island's northern half, leaving the southern coastal plain in the rain shadow. At the island's eastern end, the famous mountain "El Yunque" is covered on its top by one of the world's most lush and diversified rain forests, resulting from the fact that the precipitation is there the highest in Puerto Rico, exceeding 200 inches per year. At San Juan, some twenty miles away, it is about 65 inches. At the island's southwest tip, west of Ponce, it drops to below 30 inches. Tree ferns and orchids on the northern and central mountain slopes, mangrove swamps along the coast, cacti in the semi-arid southwest are together indicative of wide climatic variations on a relatively small island.

While Puerto Rico experienced only three truly destructive hurricanes during the 62 years from 1899 to 1961, hardly a year passes without its storm-warnings. Every year, from July through October, the island's people are acutely aware of the danger from hurricanes which they name, as if in rebuke, after the saints on whose days they occur.

WATERS

There are more than 1,000 small streams, including 45 rivers which empty into the sea, all shallow and non-navigable. There are no large lakes except those which have been created artificially by impounding surface waters for the generation of electricity and for irrigation on the semi-arid south coastal plain. In certain areas where the promotion of manufacturing seems desirable, a decided shortage of fresh water for industrial purposes has begun to be felt in recent years.

The ocean surrounding Puerto Rico supports a certain amount of local fishing to supply local needs but is generally regarded as being too deep for the kind of industrialized commercial fishing, for export of the processed catch, which flourishes on the North American Grand Banks and sustains virtually the entire economy of Iceland. Of ocean fishing, Perloff writes in his *Puerto Rico's Economic Future:* "Fish in near-by waters do not seem to be abundant. Thus far, the fishing industry has been able to supply only about 4 or 5 per cent of the local needs."

RESOURCES

THE LAND

Topographic conditions mean that only a little more than one-third of all of Puerto Rico's land surface is "arable" as the term is commonly used. For centuries the island's remarkably fertile people have battled against their country's grim physical realities to maintain what was until very recently a predominatly agrarian economy. Today the population numbers nearly 2,000 per square mile of cultivated land. Demographers like to say that the creation and maintenance of decent standards of living require some 2-½

MAP 3

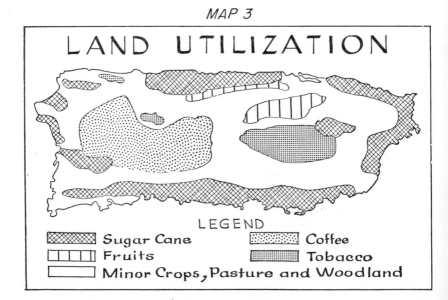

LAND UTILIZATION

LEGEND

Sugar Cane   Coffee
Fruits   Tobacco
Minor Crops, Pasture and Woodland

acres of arable land per person. Puerto Rico has 3 persons for every acre of such land, while the United States has more than 3 acres per capita.

Perloff writes as follows:

> Only a relatively small part of the island's land consists of high-productivity soils. About a quarter of the total can be considered relatively rich soil: 28.2 per cent of the land was rated "5" or above in general productivity (on a scale of "1" to "10") by the United States Department of Agriculture in its *Soil Survey of Puerto Rico,* published in 1942; a mere 6 per cent was given the top rating of "1." . . . The better lands are located chiefly in the narrow coastal, flood and inner plains, and alluvial fans. . . . Most of the island—71.2 per cent—consists of hills and mountains, the greater part of whose soils are of relatively poor quality. In general, Puerto Rico's soils are poor in nitrogen and phosphoric acid, and many of them are likewise deficient in potash and lime. As a rule, artificial fertilizers are needed to grow remunerative crops.

As discussed in greater detail in Chapter VII, the paucity of arable lands and their distribution in certain definite locations led to the growth of a cash-export agrarian economy in which every acre had to produce its maximum in profits, albeit under prevailing methods of cultivation which were often primitive. Map 3, showing land utilization in a somewhat rudimentary manner, is also a fair general picture of Puerto Rico's entire economy before 1940. Another map, showing land tenure, would show that the concentration of land in large estates is greatest in the areas of specialized cash-export crops.

Among the four principal cash crops—sugar, coffee, tobacco, and fruits—, sugar was and is by far the most important. So greatly did its production predominate over all other agricultural activities, especially after the Spanish-American War, that Puerto Rico truly developed what is known as a "one-crop" economy.

In a sense, the "blank" spaces on the land-use map, euphemistically labeled "minor crops, pasture, and woodland" but actually too rough to be farmed except in sporadic patches, represent the Puerto Rico which inspires nostalgia among poets and writers of songs. This was long the Puerto Rico of small farmers, producing food for their own sustenance and that of the cities; still earlier, it was the Puerto Rico of ox carts and pack-horses, transporting provender to markets at dawn. Today, when it is increasingly impossible for such farmers to survive in the face of economic progress and technical advances elsewhere, the "blank" areas on the land-use map are also the most fertile seed-beds for migrants to cities in the mainland United States, including New York, Chicago, and San Francisco.

PUERTO RICO AND CUBA

After the Spanish-American War, the United States became the principal, and usually the only, purchaser of Puerto Rico's sugar and such of its by-products as molasses. Until the Castro revolution led to the curtailment of Cuba's quota, only Cuba sold more sugar to the United States than did Puerto Rico, despite the fact that Cuba paid duty on its exports to the United States. Not until 1934 was the rivalry between the two controlled by the quota system, and for a time thereafter every year saw a struggle between them, through their lobbies in Washington, for favorable quota adjustments.

Differences in geographic realities favored Cuba in that rivalry and created conditions under which Cuba could afford to pay duty on its shipments to the United States while Puerto Rico could not and cannot. The republic's soils are more friable and fertile than are Puerto Rico's, more easily worked, requiring less artificial fertilization. Moreover, Cuba has far more land available. Until the Castro regime instituted its programs of land reform, Cuba's sugar industry could and did progressively abandon overworked areas and move to new lands which were still virgin as far as sugar cane was concerned. In land-poor Puerto Rico, such shifting is impossible. Because of the uneven distribution of rainfall, the sugar lands on Puerto Rico's south coast must be irrigated with water brought expensively down from the mountains; Cuba's rainfall is more evenly distributed, requiring no help from irrigation. The same mountains which in Puerto Rico are responsible for the rainfall's uneven distribution also create transportation problems. Building roads over them is an expensive matter. Cane and cane products must be transported along the coastline, thereby covering relatively greater distances than in Cuba, which has a central railroad down its middle where Puerto Rico has mountains. Even the population situation has militated economically in Cuba's favor. Short of manpower, the republic's sugar industry long imported labor at harvest time from such countries as Jamaica and Haiti, to bring in the crops and then return to their respective homes. Overcrowded Puerto Rico could not follow that pleasant practice. It had somehow to take care of its sugar workers, not only during the five harvest months but during the rest of the year as well. With all its evils of exploitation and abysmally low wages, Puerto Rico had still to pay its cane cutters more than did Cuba.

MINERAL RESOURCES

Perloff writes:

Explorations to date indicate that the island's mineral resources are scarce and generally of a low grade. It is known that a wide variety of minerals are present . . . , but there are few data relative to their composition or geology. There are abundant quantities of sand, limestone, gravel, kaolin and clay of various kinds suitable for the manufacture of cement, glass, ceramics and building materials. The island has shipped a small quantity of manganese to the mainland, but this mining operation has ceased. Silver, lead, and copper in small quantities have been discovered. Magnetic iron is found in a number of places in large quantities, but smelting and transportation difficulties have prevented development. In general, the known industrial and precious metals are not present in sufficiently concentrated and available form to justify commercial working. Mining absorbs only a small number of the employed population, usually fewer than 1800.

As far as is known, there are no economically exploitable coal or oil shale deposits, but oil exploration on a small scale is now being made. Falling water for hydroelectric power has been increasingly exploited.

FOREST PRODUCTS

The first European settlers in Puerto Rico found the island's interior covered by an exuberant forest growth, comprising, as almost everywhere in the tropics, a wide variety of trees, from the hardest to the softest, the heaviest to the lightest. Mahogany, for instance, was abundant, and San Juan's old buildings still contain a large quantity of hand-hewn beams of hardwoods, resistant to termites, all but indestructible. With time, however, the mounting pressure of populations against resources stripped most of the land of its timber, so giving rise to soil erosion which has, among other ills, resulted in serious silting in several of the reservoirs for hydroelectric development. Today the limited forest lands produce an insignificant amount of lumber as well as wood for charcoal. Virtually all wood for construction and other purposes, totaling about $4 million annually, must now be imported

PHYSICAL PROBLEMS
AND INDICATED SOLUTIONS

A distressing physical reality is always made worse by undue concern on the part of those who must cope with it. A society remaking itself grows skeptical about its former pessimism; it comes to regard its geographic handicaps as human problems rather than divine punishments. Similarly, the value of a natural resource depends only in part on its inherent nature. It is also determined in large measure by what it means to the society which must use it, by that society's determination, its imagination, its inventiveness, its economic, political, and other abilities to make the most of that resource.

CLIMATE

Until fairly recently, the pessimism inspired by Puerto Rico's natural poverty was augmented by the low regard in which too many eminent scholars held the world's tropical regions. In 1936 a distinguished geographer belonging to the Huntington school of climatic determinism came to Puerto Rico to teach in the university's summer school. In his seminars he intoned that the tropical climate robs people of energy and that Puerto Rico could therefore never amount to much except under the guidance and management of energetic men from the more stimulating "temperate" regions. Some of his students believed him and for a time prated his nonsense as proof of their own erudition. Not until they had begun energetically to take hold of their own affairs did the Puerto Ricans make the agreeable discovery that the artificial, devitalizing, unhealthful social climate of colonialism, rather than the natural climate, tends to rob tropical peoples of their energy.

Today the climate is regarded as an asset rather than a liability. Good climate, fine scenery, and gentle, hospitable, intelligent people constitute resources which can be sold to vacationing visitors. The tourist industry, now one of the island's most important, began to get under way about 1950, with the construction of fine hotels and the inauguration of a vigorous program of promotion. For some years the Commonwealth's advertisements in the states pronounced the climate to be "the nearest thing to paradise a man will ever see," an exuberant exaggeration which was dropped only after an ill-natured critic had called Madison Avenue's attention to the fact that mixing theology with advertising is in decidedly bad taste.

Every climatic reality, of course, poses its own problems of adjustment in a developing society. For instance, while hurricanes may correctly be regarded as "acts of God," the former, exaggerated losses suffered from them need not be. The threat of hurricanes calls for crop insurance, especially in the coffee regions whose trees are peculiarly susceptible to storm damage and where such insurance is today an established fact, provided by the government. The destruction of homes, especially among the rural poor who have long regarded the potential losses of their often flimsy little houses with a despairing fatalism, calls for the widespread creation of concrete structures, hurricane-proof, fireproof, vermin-proof, and at low cost, for which Puerto Rico is today world famous. The destructive floods which often accompany hurricanes pose problems in flood control which the government has not yet solved but of which it is thoroughly aware.

FISHING

The poverty of marine life in surrounding waters, and especially of edible fish, which led Perloff to point out that only about 4 or 5 per cent of the island's needs in fish and other seafoods are met by local fishermen, is only in part absolute. Some of it stems from antiquated points of view which are today being challenged.

While it is true that Puerto Rico lacks adequate plants for processing and freezing the fishermen's catches, and while it is equally true that the surrounding waters do not offer sufficient marine wealth to warrant the installation of such plants on an industrial scale, it is also true that the development of "deep freeze" facilities in relatively small units has proved a boon to the island's fishermen. Their markets have been expanded considerably by the installation of such equipment in their own quarters as well as in restaurants and hotels.

Moreover, the fishermen's own boats and gear have hitherto been relatively poor and antiquated. In recent years, however, the Government Development Bank, discussed in Chapter VIII, which lends money to investors for the purchase of industrial machinery, has inaugurated a program for making capital loans to fishermen for the purpose of acquiring motorized boats and more adequate catching equipment.

The promotion of sport fishing, for which Puerto Rico's waters offer splendid opportunities, was undertaken some years ago as an activity to interest vacationers and to help boost the tourist industry. It is today a thriving business which attracts amateur and professional sports fishermen from far and wide. The resulting closer acquaintance with the sea and its offerings has begun to result in growing doubts as to whether or not the former pessimism toward commercial fishing was fully justified. The phenomenal recent rise of spear-fishing, for which some of the Puerto Rican grounds are said to be among the world's best, has resulted not only in a corresponding increase of Puerto Rican "lobsters" (actually large crayfish) for Puerto Rican tables, but has again created the closer acquaintance with the island's waters which in turn tends to modify the former more or less dogmatic pessimism.

Meanwhile, inland streams and reservoirs are being stocked with fish. Fishing in the hydroelectric reservoirs and elsewhere is growing in popularity and importance, while also calling for accelerated public-health measures to combat bilharzia. This incurable disease, which affects the liver, is spread by a fresh-water snail and is picked up by humans who swim or wade in the waters in which the snail is prevalent. An energetic program to eliminate a dangerous pest must here go hand in hand with another to improve health by augmenting the available supply of protein foods. Both are today integral parts of the government's far-flung program.

PROSPECTING

The experiences of many amateur and professional fishermen constitute a kind of marine prospecting which leads, in one way or another, to revisions of former gloomy estimates. Similarly, it is today being realized that the island's poverty in land resources may not be as great as was once supposed.

For instance, the long-rooted "knowledge" that Puerto Rico has no exploitable petroleum deposits is now being tested. While prospecting for oil is too expensive a matter to be undertaken by a government which is still, despite its progress of recent decades, relatively poor (Puerto Rico's per capita average annual income remains less than half that of Mississippi, America's poorest state), there is no reason why private venture-capital should not be encouraged to engage in that activity. In recent years a private company has drilled for oil under a government concession. It has met with some rather encouraging results, and the mere fact that it is willing to spend its money on the search indicates possibilities that the former pessimism regarding that extremely important commodity may have been ill-founded or at least exaggerated.

The current interest in the re-examination of available resources led a few years ago to the discovery of workable marble deposits of good quality. The quarrying and sale of marble have begun to constitute a new and relatively important industry.

The fact that supplies of fresh surface water are scarce in certain areas, so hampering industrial development in those areas, has recently called for a systematic survey of ground waters, carried out jointly by the Puerto Rican government and the United States Geological Survey.

FOREST PRODUCTS

While it is still true that Puerto Rico has long since lost the forest resources which might otherwise support a commercial lumbering industry, it is also true that something is now being done about that situation. Forest reserves on the mountain tops, and especially on those which offer little or no opportunity for agriculture, are now being expanded and carefully administered by the Commonwealth government as well as by the federal.

Experiences with the "yagruma" tree, whose picturesque large leaves, green on top and white on the bottom, may occasionally be seen for sale in New York as tropical curios, point to other possible solutions of the forest-products problem. A fast-growing tree with wood so light that it approaches balsa, the yagruma was long regarded as a weed, an almost ineradicable pest whose sole value lay in the fact that the Puerto Ricans could amuse themselves by calling two-faced persons "yagruma leaves." A few years ago, however, a private company established a factory near Ponce for macerating the yagruma wood, treating it chemically, and converting it into a synthetic lumber which is easily worked, fireproof, vermin-proof, and considerably less expensive than is natural lumber. To landowners within economic hauling distance of the factory, the yagruma is now an asset rather than the liability it once was.

When technology arrives at the point where all natural woods, mixed indiscriminately, may be ground up, treated, and converted economically into synthetic lumbers, Puerto Rico's remaining for-est-stands will acquire new economic importance.

POLITICAL PROBLEMS

The effectiveness of developmental planning is always at least in part determined by the political climate within which it functions. In some Latin American nations which have recently emerged from despotism, the very word "planning" is still anathema, simply because the activity had formerly been fostered by their dictators to further their own ends. The pessimism of Puerto Rico's young planners during the 1930's was justified in part by the fact that colonial subjects, while they can dream, scheme, and actually plan for the improvement of their lives, lack the political power to translate their shining dreams into action.

OBSTACLES TO INDUSTRY

It was obvious, even in 1935, that while Puerto Rico's economic structure was too small to provide anything but an extremely narrow base for industrialization, *something* could conceivably be done. However, when the planners of those days examined the political and related economic scene within which industrialization would have to take place, their resulting pessimism led them largely to prepare basic reports on the defeatist theme of "Obstacles to Industry in Puerto Rico." The thread of that theme wove its way through studies of the tariff situation as it affected the island, of the political control exercised by the sugar industry and the large land-owners, of the cost of shipping in United States bottoms, of "unfair" competition from the mainland United States, over which the "exploited" colony of Puerto Rico had no control.

The many and recurring complaints, mounting in essence to a wail against the very institution of colonialism, were buttressed by meticulous, scholarly studies which formed a valuable body of inquiry into colonialism's very nature. What happened to most of them is not known today. One, however, Estéban Bird's scathing report on the exploitative sugar industry, had a revealing history.

Commissioned in 1936 by the Federal Reconstruction Administration, it was, on completion, suppressed by that organization's officials. However, it was later used as evidence in litigation over land tenure and other points of disagreement with the sugar industry. Having so become a public document, it was published triumphantly by the new government in 1941, as the first of its basic, factual, revolutionary studies.

THE PROBLEM OF DUMPING

While the Reconstruction Administration did build a cement factory and turn it over to the Puerto Rican government, which very soon paid for it out of profits, the general prospects for successful industrialization were dismal, in part because even in those years Puerto Rico was the second largest market for United States exports in the Americas, being topped only by Canada. Hard hit by the depression, United States exporters were not inclined to let that market diminish. The result was a forbidding social-economic climate for the investment of capital and effort in manufacturing. The various American soap companies, for instance, sold so large an amount of their products that they maintained 22 representatives in Puerto Rico alone. But when a Puerto Rican began to make soap locally, the price of soap from the mainland dropped to such low levels that the local enterprise, having no lasting power, was forced out of business.

Dumping and the manipulation of freight rates were, in those years, used by North American shippers to protect their Puerto Rican markets and to keep the island subservient to mainland United States interests. Moreover, there was nothing unique about the fact that those interests were in effect in league with the powerful, feudal, large landowners in the matter of preventing (or at least deterring) industrial and general development designed to improve standards of living by providing new opportunities and increasing wages. That situation was common throughout Latin America and helped to buttress the charge that the United States was a grasping, imperialist nation.

The Population Problem

PUERTO RICO is a crowded island by any definition, with a fertile population and a density per square mile resembling those of Japan and the United Kingdom, as shown by Map 4. The census of 1960 gave it 2,349,544 inhabitants, or some 682 per square mile. Its rate of increase has been so large that horrified demographers have long pointed it out as one of the world's most awful examples of the current "population explosion."

In a manner which has become fashionable in recent decades, Kingsley Davis wrote in 1952 that the "rate of natural increase——the excess of births over deaths in relation to population—has . . . recently been one of the highest in the world. The average rate for the decade 1942-51 is so high that, if continued without migration, it would double the population in approximately 26 years. This would give the island nearly 9,000,000 inhabitants by the end of the century, nearly 18,000,000 in 75 years, and soon there would be standing room only."

POPULATION AND ECONOMICS

Davis realized that current trends such as rising standards of living, improved and extended education, population movements from the rural to the urban areas, and the growth of a new middle class presage "a period of declining fertility." However, a glance at the island's vital statistics still results in some rather startling disclosures. Table 1 indicates the demographic changes between 1940 and 1960, together with the per capita average annual income as an index of rising standards of living.

The year 1947 was inserted in the table because it was, demographically speaking, a climax year and a turning point, when the

Table 1

	1940	1947	1950	1960
Total Population	1,869,000	2,113,000	2,210,703	2,349,544
Density per Square Mile	543	612	641	682
Births per Thousand	39.0	43.9	39.6	31.5
Deaths per Thousands	18.2	12.6	10.5	6.6
Difference	20.8	31.3	29.1	24.9
Life Expectancy in Years	46	46	61	68
Per Capita Average Annual Income	$121	$254	$279	$587

birth rate reached an all-time high. The year also marked a turning point in economic development and consequent changes in social conditions. World War II had impeded development, but now, with a Puerto Rican in the governor's seat for the first time in history, with the time only a year off when the island's people could elect their own governor, and with the war fortunately over, the time came for taking stock, for the reappraisal of old policies and the establishment of new, for an energetic fresh start.

With reference exclusively to Dr. Davis' "rate of natural increase, the excess of births over deaths . . . ," the table seems to show that in 1960 Puerto Rico was worse off than in 1940, though not as badly as in 1947 and 1950. In 1960, 31.5 persons were born for every 6.6 who died, a difference of 24.9 as compared with 20.8 twenty years earlier. Moreover, the 24.9 of 1960 had to eat three meals a day for an average span of 68 years, while in 1940 such meals had some-how to be provided throughout only 46 years. The figures bear out Harvey Perloff's description of Puerto Rico as being "in an Alice in Wonderland situation, where one has to run very fast merely to stay in the same place." In his study of Puerto Rico's prospects, Perloff also expressed fear of "the disturbing tendency for economic gains to be swallowed up by continuing rapid growth of the population in areas which are already densely populated and economically un-derdeveloped."

BIRTH RATES AND STANDARDS OF LIVING

Dramatically, the table illustrates something that population ex-perts have long known, though some of them are reluctant to ad-

MAP 4

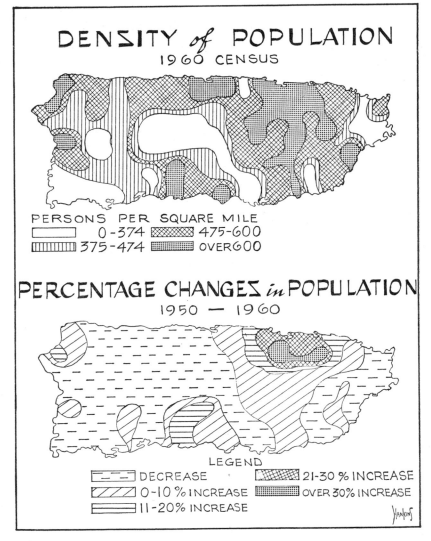

DENSITY *of* POPULATION

1960 CENSUS

PERSONS PER SQUARE MILE

0-374		475-600	
375-474		OVER 600	

PERCENTAGE CHANGES *in* POPULATION

1950 — 1960

LEGEND

DECREASE		21-30% INCREASE
0-10% INCREASE		OVER 30% INCREASE
11-20% INCREASE		

Hankins

mit it. Among the latter are those who proclaim that the United States should refuse all aid for economic development to poor and crowded countries unless the people of those countries first consent to practice birth control. Not only do rising standards of living mean declining birth rates, but there seems to be considerable evidence that *only* through the improvements of living standards can the current "population explosion" be brought to an end. The 24.9 persons per thousand who in 1960 had to eat regularly for some 68 years had an average per capita annual income of $587 with which to arrange the matter (the figure rose to $621 in 1961), while the 20.8 of 1940 had only $121 per year for the purpose of surviving a mere 46 years. Between 1940 and 1950, the total increase of Puerto Rico's population was 18.3 per cent, while the corresponding increase of the island's gross product, from $287 million to $751 million, was over 160 per cent. Between 1950 and 1960, the population increased from 2,210,703 to 2,349,544 or only 6.3 per cent, while the gross product, soaring to $1,438 million, rose by 110 per cent. The figures here given are in current dollars, but even after corrections have been made for the dollar's depreciation, they are still impressive and tend to mitigate Perloff's fears that economic gains might be swallowed up by population increases. Obviously, barring a disaster, Puerto Rico is heading for a balance between its population and the economy supporting it.

DEMOGRAPHIC BEHAVIOR

Although a society's demographic behavior is so complex a matter that it is all but impossible to separate the many and varied interacting forces for scrutiny, some of Puerto Rico's modern social trends can bear brief discussion in relation to the so-called "population problem."

MIGRATION

As mentioned in Chapter II, the Puerto Ricans have traditionally, through the centuries and after being threatened with the death penalty for attempts to leave the island and move to Peru, clung to their land with an almost fierce passion. Seafaring and a restless urge for migration were not among their culture traits, in part because in the old days they were more docile than they seem to be today, and paid attention when their priests virtually forbade them to leave. They stayed at home and pitted their famous fertility against poverty and fatal adversities such as famines and epidemics. The population grew by fits and starts, in part through biological increase, in part through immigration.

The first outward movement of any significance occurred during the 1890's, to Hawaii, which needed field hands in its sugar industry. Today, the Puerto Rican colony there numbers about 10,000. Early in the twentieth century sporadic efforts were made to recruit Puerto Ricans for agricultural work in the States, but they were unhappy there. Coming from a land which knows virtually no racial discrimination, they found it difficult to adjust to the racism of the United States. A trickle of migrants, most of them to the continental United States though some to the Virgin Islands and a very few to various Latin American republics, began to flow out after World War I. The 1930 census showed Puerto Ricans in all of the 48 states, and by 1940 New York City had 63,000 of them. However, it was not until after World War II that the stream of emigrants began to have an appreciable effect on Puerto Rico's population problem. In 1947, 35,000 left the island. The number rose fitfully to an all-time high of 75,000 in 1953, and then declined again to 14,000 in 1961. The following year more Puerto Ricans returned to their island than left it. New York, with some 750,000 Puerto Ricans, is today by far the largest Puerto Rican city. Since most of the migrants are in the most fertile age-group and many of them come from Puerto Rico's rural areas where people have more children than in the cities, their departure undoubtedly affected the island's birth rate, as the current drop in emigration will probably mean a temporary rise in that rate.

THE PSYCHOLOGY OF MIGRATION

The reasons for so sudden and massive an exodus at precisely the time when the island experienced its greatest improvement are many and interrelated. The very fact that the modern revolution

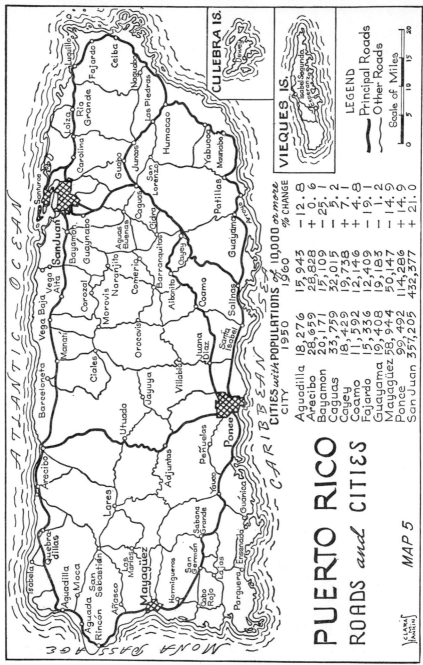

PUERTO RICO
ROADS and CITIES

MAP 5

	CITIES with POPULATIONS of 10,000 or more		
CITY	1950	1960	% CHANGE
Aguadilla	18,276	15,943	− 12.8
Arecibo	28,659	28,828	+ 0.6
Bayamon	20,171	15,109	− 25.1
Caguas	33,759	32,015	− 5.2
Cayey	18,429	19,738	+ 7.1
Coamo	11,592	12,146	+ 4.8
Fajardo	15,336	12,409	− 19.1
Guayama	19,408	19,183	− 1.2
Mayagüez	58,944	50,147	− 14.9
Ponce	99,492	114,286	+ 14.9
San Juan	357,205	432,377	+ 21.0

CULEBRA IS.

VIEQUES IS.

LEGEND
Principal Roads
Other Roads
Scale of Miles
0 5 10 15 20

ATLANTIC OCEAN

CARIBBEAN SEA

MONA PASSAGE

52

was in a large measure psychological, with the former lethargy giving way to hope and self-confidence, meant that many Puerto Ricans now gained the courage and the faith in themselves to strike out on their own in search of better economic opportunities than they could find at home. Gradually throughout the United States' regime, and more rapidly during World Wars I and II, knowledge of the world beyond replaced a former deep suspicion toward strange frontiers. Moreover, the Church, which had for centuries opposed emigration, has in recent decades lost its former hold on the island's people, most of whom today regard themselves as still being Catholics even though they don't pay as much attention as they once did to what their priests and bishops tell them.

At the present time, however, the consensus in Puerto Rico is that emigration will continue to fall as the island's economy continues to improve.

GROWTH OF THE CITIES

The movement to the continental United States is an aspect of an intense, restless larger migration through which, inevitably, the Puerto Rican people are redistributing themselves. The "population movement from the rural to the urban areas" mentioned by Kingsley Davis has continued without interruption during the decade since he published his study. People are abandoning large sections of countryside and moving to the cities. Under the impact of modern trucking, a number of small towns in the interior are losing their former importance as centers for transportation and trade, and with it are losing much of their former population. Map 5 indicates the general trend of internal migrations between 1950 and 1960, with large areas showing declines in population and others indicating various degrees of growth.

However, not all the cities grew during that decade. Of the eleven largest, only five increased in population. San Juan grew by 21.0 per cent, Ponce 14.9, Cayey 7.1, Coamo 4.8, and Arecibo 0.6; all the rest decreased. The third largest, Mayaguez, lost 14.9 per cent between 1950 and 1960, for a number of reasons which have an interesting bearing on population movements. Once a center of the

sweatshop needlework trade, the city lost a large share of that trade
to Japan and the Philippines, in part because of the passage of mini-
mum wage legislation. Its seaport, though small, was formerly of
considerable importance, especially for handling bagged sugar and
gasoline. But the sugar industry has abandoned bags and is now
shipping all its raw suger in bulk, through four specially constructed ports, while two new refineries on the island, receiving
and processing crude oil, have eliminated gasoline from the commodities handled at the port. Such economic shifts, together with
the fact that the highway serving Mayaguez was long antiquated
and inadequate, account for the city's recent losses in population
which may, however, soon be reversed as a result of the government's promotional actions. As stated in Chapter II, an international free trade zone has been established, together with two
canneries for tuna fish. The road is being improved, as is the port,
and Mayaguez may soon turn the corner and again become a thriving industrial city.

URBAN GROWTH AND FERTILITY

The growth of the cities inevitably affects the fertility pattern, for
a number of reasons which are interrelated in a complex manner.
Suffice it here to say that in the country, no matter how poor life is,
children are often needed as cheap labor; the poorer the life the
more they are needed, and the earlier they die, the sooner they must
be replaced. But life is different in the cities, more crowded, more
expensive, while Puerto Rico's modern child-labor laws preclude
the use of children as supplementary bread-winners. Moreover,
it is easier to send them to school, while their parents themselves
are exposed to a number of educational experiences. The general
rule that "it is only when people begin to worry about sending their
children to college that they also worry about having fewer," applies
with many variations to life in the cities.

THE HOUSING PROBLEM

The growth of certain cities creates serious problems for the
housing authorities. The so-called "population problem" discussed

by demographers divides itself on examination into a large series of regional "population problems," some of them calling for planned efforts to reverse the outflow while others demand drastic action for handling the inflow. Not only relatively, but also in an absolute sense, Puerto Rico is taking more advantage of federal aid in housing than is any state of the union. Throughout the metropolitan area surrounding San Juan, great new developments are being built by private companies to receive those who are reasonably well off and members of the new middle class, which is growing rapidly as a result of industrialization. At the same time, however, the government's Urban Renewal and Housing Corporation finds it all but impossible to build decent, low-cost public housing projects rapidly enough to keep pace with the influx of poor people who squat on all the areas they can find, build miserable wooden shacks, create new slums, and are often difficult to dislodge once they have established themselves.

In the government projects, people pay rent, not according to the sizes of their apartments, but according to their ability. A large but poor family may live in a three bedroom apartment for some $6.50 per month, while a small but richer family pays up to $30.00 for the adjoining apartment with only one bedroom. Moreover, when a family's income rise above $2,500 per year, it is no longer eligible to rent a government apartment and must move out.

THE "FORGOTTEN" INCOME GROUP

Two groups within the lower income brackets suffer from that system. At one end are those who cannot be accommodated because facilities cannot be prepared rapidly enough to take care of them. At the other are those whose incomes, while too high to permit their renting public housing, are yet too low for the purchase of even the smallest of privately built homes at the most generous rates of financing. As far as housing is concerned, those whose incomes are between $2,500 and $3,500 are said to belong to the "forgotten" group. The situation has given rise to much planning and remedial action within the realm of "aided self-help," which is more difficult in the cities, demanding more exacting standards than in the country. Of the several proposals and experiments, the "core type" house seems to be the most successful. In that program, the Housing Corporation provides the floor, columns and roof, while the family finishes the rest of the house under self-help. Facilities are provided for paying for the house over periods which range from five to twenty years, according to the family's income.

BIRTH CONTROL AND THE CHURCH

The trends mentioned above, plus those in education and public health dealt with in Chapter IX, tend inevitably to reduce the birth rate and were responsible for the fact that the total rate of growth, 18.1 per cent during the decade 1940-1950, had gone down to 6.3 per cent during the following ten years. The mechanics by which the birth rate is reduced are sterilization and contraception. Though the government itself, for obvious reasons, does not participate in such activities, it does permit, under a law passed before Muñoz Marín started the revolution in 1940, the sterilization of women whose lives may for one reason or another be endangered by having more children, while also permitting the dissemination of contraceptive information and materials.

Sterilization has become quite popular. According to a statement issued by an appalled bishop in 1960, it has by now reached a rate of some 17,000 women per year, with a trickle of men (not mentioned by the prelate) thrown in for good measure. The bishops themselves, though they are unhappy about the matter, must be careful not to rail against it too diligently. One episcopal letter denouncing it, read some ten years ago in all the island's Catholic churches, aroused so much interest of the "this is wonderful, where can we find out more?" type that the rate at which women were being sterilized at their own request (there is no forced sterilization) was said to rise as a result of it from a thousand to ten thousand per year. Many upper-class women, too, request sterilization after they have had two or three children; the culture trait of large families is rapidly disappearing.

The mass experiments conducted by the Puerto Rican Family Planning Association, whose executive director is Mrs. Celestina

Zalduondo, have begun to attract world attention. Working with thousands of volunteers, and with the help of a barrage of educational materials, this group tested thoroughly the now-famous contraceptive pill, taken orally. The test ran for a period of years, proved the pill effective and showed no negative side-results, such as the permanent loss of fertility which some medical men had feared. It was largely as a result of that work that the United States Food and Drug Administration, in 1960, approved the pill's marketing for contraceptive purposes throughout the United States.

THE CHURCH AND POLITICS

Naturally, such activities and the declining birth rate distress the Catholic hierarchy, at least on a local level, and so create more problems for the government. During the crucial election year of 1960, the Church, for that and other reasons, organized its own political party, the Christian Action Party, and established it through petitions bearing far more signatures than the required ten per cent of the votes cast in the previous election. Blaming Governor Muñoz Marín, albeit unjustly, for the current trend toward birth control, Puerto Rico's bishops made political platforms out of all their churches by ordering the reading of several pastoral letters which in the beginning urged the faithful to join the Christian Action Party and later proclaimed that voting for Muñoz Marín and his party would be a sin which might or might not—the issue was never truly clarified—lead to excommunication.

The net result, in a society which is more than 80 per cent Catholic, was surprising. Muñoz Marín's party polled 58 per cent of the total vote cast, the Christian Action party only 6.6 per cent, while 32.3 per cent went to the Republican Party favoring statehood for Puerto Rico, and a mere 3.1 per cent to the party favoring independence.

GENERAL CONSIDERATIONS

POPULATION DENSITY AND ECONOMICS

All the trends dealt with above, plus education, public health, and many others, interacting in a complex fashion, tend to show

that the term "over-population" is more or less meaningless when
gauged by mere numbers and in relation only to the land area. The
term "land" is itself relatively meaningless when discussed out of
the context of the uses to which it is put. The degree of any
country's "over-population" can be measured only in terms of relative poverty. As related in Chapter II, the settlers who comprised
Puerto Rico's Spanish population when Pizarro and Almagro conquered Peru showed by their eagerness to leave the island and get
in on the Peruvian loot that they regarded Puerto Rico as being already "over-populated" in the sixteenth century, with only some
three hundred Spanish settlers and a population density of less than
one tenth of a white man (the Indians didn't count) per square
mile, compared to today's 682. In 1940, the island was far more
"crowded" in the social sense, with 1,869,000 inhabitants earning an
average of $121 per year each, than it is today (1961), with 2,344,-
544, earning $621.

MAN, A CREATIVE ANIMAL

By his spark of divinity, man is above all a creative animal whose
creative urges cannot be denied or suppressed; they can be merely
channeled and re-channeled as opportunities are created. Deprive
him, through the political and economic workings of such institutions as feudalism and colonialism, of the opportunity to create a
better life for himself and his children, and he is virtually forced to
apply his creative energies to the one channel left for him, the
biological. Indeed, during the unhappy days of the one-crop sugar
economy, many of the island's "best" people, their bread buttered
on the sugar side, insisted that Puerto Rico's only trouble consisted
of its people's exuberant fertility; check it, they argued, and the island could become a veritable paradise. Perhaps that is why it was
the Republican Party, the political organ of the powerful feudal
land-owners, which during the 1930's passed the law permitting
sterilization for which Muñoz Marín is today being blamed.

The more fanatical and sensational of our currently fashionable
demographers, who interpret rates of increase and population den-
sities as harbingers of imminent doom, are actually telling each

other and their readers that the modern world's greatest trouble is that it is too full of improvident foreigners who stubbornly refuse to practice birth control for the purpose of safeguarding our high American standards of living, which they have never been permitted to enjoy.

HANSON'S LAW

Actually, while the land and its resources are fixed and immutable, the economy, meaning the uses to which the land is put, is flexible and can be expanded, how far nobody can estimate. Puerto Rico again bears out what has come to be called "Hanson's Law," viz: "It is never a land which is over-populated, in terms of inhabitants per square mile; it is always an economy, in terms of square meals per inhabitant."

V   *Political Evolution*

Luis Muñoz Rivera, father of the present governor and one of Puerto Rico's outstanding heroes, sailed for Spain in 1896 as head of a committee to demand self-government. He returned with Puerto Rico's "autonomy" in his pocket, including virtual self-government in local matters and a voice in shaping Spain's foreign affairs as they affected the island. The Spanish decree granting that relative freedom was signed in Spain on November 25, 1897. The new home-rule government took charge in San Juan, after due elections, on February 9, 1898. Spain declared war upon the United States on April 21. The following day the San Juan government affirmed Puerto Rico's solidarity with the mother country and called on all Puerto Ricans to fight valiantly against the Americanos. After General Nelson A. Miles had landed with his troops at Guánica on the south coast on July 25, he issued a proclamation of friendship for Puerto Rico's people and announced that the United States did not intend to alter the island's laws and customs.

Widely hailed as liberators, encountering virtually no opposition, the American troops required 19 days to occupy all parts of the island. They had arrived barely in the nick of time to establish our claim to Puerto Rico. Spain was now permitted to capitulate, and armed hostilities ceased a mere 18 days after the landing.

THE UNITED STATES MILITARY GOVERNMENT

Puerto Rico now obtained a military government. Some decades after Puerto Rico was formally ceded to the United States by the terms of the Treaty of Paris, the Nationalist leader, Pedro Albizu Campos, was to claim that the treaty, having never been ratified by the Puerto Ricans, was invalid as far as the latter were concerned and that they were therefore entitled to independence. Whatever the claim's validity, it is true that what little independence they *had* attained some five months before General Miles' landing had been taken away again.

One election for the purpose of choosing municipal officials was held under rules laid down by the military governor, General George W. Davis. The universal suffrage adopted during the brief period of autonomy was abolished; now the vote was confined to men, 21 years of age and older, who were either property owners or literate. Only literate owners of property were allowed to run for office. Since more than 80 per cent of the Puerto Ricans were illiterate, the disenfranchisement was massive. The total vote was 51,649, in a population of approximately a million, and its casting required more than three months. The process became known as "The election of a hundred days." Starting in Adjuntas in July 1899 and moving thence from town to town, district to district, in alphabetical order, the balloting finally wound up in Yauco in January 1900. The campaign speeches and actual voting were marked by violent passions, inflamed emotions, and physical clashes. Despite a steady stream of restrictive and regulatory decrees which General Davis shot from the Fortaleza at the bewildered population, United States troops found it difficult to keep a semblance of order. The net result was that the election gave the Puerto Ricans a reputation in the United States, assiduously spread by the governor, of being a backward, unruly lot, not ready for democracy, unfit for self-government.

THE FORAKER ACT

On April 12, 1900, President McKinley signed the Foraker Act providing for a civil government for Puerto Rico. The chief executive was to be the governor, appointed by the President; members of his eleven-man Executive Council were similarly appointed by the President. In a two-chamber legislature, the executive council became the upper house; the lower house of 35 members was elected by the people. The organic act, Puerto Rico's first constitution under the American flag, drafted unilaterally by the United

States Congress with no Puerto Rican having a voice in its preparation, provided for a Supreme Court of five members, all of them appointed by the President. In Washington, Puerto Rico was to be represented by an elected "resident commissioner," who sat in the House of Representatives, where he had a voice but no vote. The Congress, moreover, reserved the right to annul any legislation passed in and by Puerto Rico which might slip past the governor's veto power; it also reserved the right to legislate for Puerto Rico.

Senator Foraker's grim piece of legislative legerdemain said nothing about the citizens' rights, did not, in other words, include a Bill of Rights. The island's people were designated "citizens of Puerto Rico" (but not of the United States), placing them in the anomalous position of being citizens of a country which did not exist, of a society which had virtually no trace of self-government. Only the act's fiscal aspects pleased the Puerto Ricans. Coming within the United States' tariff structure, the island was to have free trade with the ruling country, without having to contribute to the United States treasury. Customs duties, for instance, collected by the United States on foreign goods imported into Puerto Rico, were to be turned over to the Puerto Rican government instead of going to Washington. Under the principle of "no taxation without representation," Puerto Rico still does not contribute to the federal treasury. Customs duties collected on the island are still turned over to Puerto Rico, as are excise taxes on rum and cigars. The Puerto Ricans, as long as they remain on their island, do not pay federal income taxes. Industries in Puerto Rico do not pay the corporate profits tax of 52 per cent which they would have to pay if Puerto Rico were a federated state.

COLONIALISM UNDER CIVIL GOVERNMENT

The civil government provided for in the Foraker Act took hold May 1, 1900. Of the Executive Council's eleven members, six were also heads of government departments and so formed the governor's cabinet, though all were appointed by the President. All of the six who formed the cabinet were "continentals," Americans who knew no Spanish and knew little if anything about Puerto Rico. Only the other five, who had only advisory power, were prominent Puerto Ricans, belonging to various local political parties.

Within the framework of such arrangements, the local political debate came to be centered largely, not on governmental measures and policies which the Puerto Ricans lacked the powers to formulate and enforce, but on alternatives to colonialism. One party wanted federated statehood, another labored for independence, a third talked about a kind of autonomy under which the Puerto Ricans could preserve their cultural identity with no danger of being "absorbed" as second-class North Americans. Parties came and went; they formed alliances, broke up, disappeared, and sprang up again in new forms. Elections, reputedly struggles over matters of high principles, were to a large extent struggles over municipal positions and for partisan voices in matters pertaining to patronage and the budget.

GOOD GOVERNORS AND BAD

Woodrow Wilson was elected president in 1912, and Puerto Rico felt the change immediately. A "good" governor, Arthur Yager, with liberal leanings and great sympathy for Puerto Rican aspirations, was sent to San Juan, and for the first time under the Foraker Act two Puerto Ricans were appointed to cabinet positions. The people of Puerto Rico were jubilant until Wilson was succeeded by Harding and Yager was succeeded by the "bad" governor, J. Montgomery Reily, who waved the American flag, stood for no nonsense, punished all professions of Liberalism, and cracked down on those who were even suspected of being for the island's independence. It taught the political leaders the important lesson that it didn't pay to go along too openly with any colonial governor, however good he was, lest a bad successor later practice reprisals.

THE PUERTO RICANS BECOME UNITED STATES CITIZENS

After World War I broke out in Europe in 1914, Wilson recommended to Congress that relations with Puerto Rico and the Philippine Islands be improved as a matter of national security.

The so-called Jones bill, providing for changes in Puerto Rico's governmental structure, was presented in the House of Representatives on January 20, 1916. After much debate and some vicissitudes, it became law on March 2 of the following year. It provided for the separation, in Puerto Rico, of executive powers from the legislative by the creation of an elected senate as the legislature's upper house. It also offered United States citizenship to the Puerto Ricans, stipulating that every Puerto Rican voter step before a magistrate and state whether he wanted to become an American citizen or remain what he was, a "citizen of Puerto Rico." The franchise for local elections was reserved for those who chose to become American citizens, though they had no vote in national elections.

Today, as a result of the Jones Act, Puerto Ricans enjoy all the civil rights of American citizenship. They can come and go freely to and within the United States, and are fully protected by United States laws, while still not contributing to the federal treasury. However, they lack political citizenship. They can not vote for the President or for voting members of Congress, although, by affiliating with the Republican or Democratic parties, they can and do send delegations to national conventions to vote for the nomination of presidential candidates. Only through being a citizen of a federated state can an American be a voting citizen of the United States. Any Puerto Rican who moves to New York or Chicago, establishes residence there and remains the length of time required for becoming a citizen of New York or Illinois, thereby automatically gains political United States citizenship, can participate in national elections, and begins to pay federal as well as state income taxes.

In Puerto Rico, the citizenship provisions of the Jones Act stirred considerable debate. A number of leaders thought that it would cloud the issue of eventual independence. However, sovereign independence is still legally possible for the Puerto Ricans, who have been assured that all they need to attain it is to vote for it in a plebiscite. If ever they do ask for it, and Congress then grants it, every Puerto Rican voter will again have to step before a magistrate to express his choice between United States and Puerto Rican citizenship.

The new organic act improved matters considerably, though the increased self-government provided by it proved more or less hollow as long as an appointed governor retained veto power over the legislature's acts and controlled patronage through his cabinet, the members of which continued to be appointed by the President. Continuing to be relatively powerless in the management of their own affairs, the Puerto Ricans also continued to talk and act on behalf of greater "freedom," meaning anything from federated statehood, through the "free, associated state" status that the island has today, to complete independence.

WHAT IS FREEDOM?

In 1927, a commission went to Washington to argue for the Puerto Ricans' right to elect their own governor, responsible to the Puerto Rican people rather than to the President and Congress of the United States. The commission accomplished nothing; it was not even received by President Coolidge. Lindbergh visited Puerto Rico early in 1928, was treated with great honor and enthusiasm, and was asked to give to President Coolidge, on his return, a legislative petition for greater "freedom." The resolution delivered to him by Lindbergh, plus a cable sent to him directly, seemed to irritate Coolidge. In a long letter addressed to Governor Towner, he explained in effect that the Puerto Ricans had "never had it so good," that they already had more freedom than ever in their history, that the several United States governments on the island, military as well as civil, had accomplished a lot, that Puerto Rico's trade had risen steadily under the American flag and management, that the Puerto Ricans did not know how to count their blessings, and that they should be grateful and stop all that talk about more freedom.

The Coolidge letter stirred up great resentment in Puerto Rico, but also led to clarification of what various Puerto Ricans and parties meant by greater freedom. It was during this period that the term "Free Associated State" was coined, meaning a political entity completely free to govern itself within the framework of the United States, under the American flag and within the American financial structure. At the same time, however, Puerto Rico's Republican Party, which was allied with that in the United States, and the Socialist Party, allied with the American Federation of Labor, advocated federated statehood as the solution for Puerto Rico's ills, while a firebrand named Pedro Albizu Campos took charge of the so-called Nationalist Party and campaigned for complete independence.

THE RISE OF TERRORISM

Albizu toured a number of Latin American republics, preached hatred for the Yanqui Imperialists, and worked up much sympathy for what he described as the stricken, oppressed, exploited, Latin American Puerto Rico. In several countries at various local levels, and in Castro's Cuba on a national level, he is still regarded as Puerto Rico's greatest modern hero and leader. His plan was to go to the League of Nations with a plea for independence, backed by support from Latin America and a mandate from Puerto Rico's voters. Returning to his home island, he began to make fiery speeches, attacking the United States as an interloper and demanding independence. People flocked to him from far and wide and applauded his speeches enthusiastically. But they failed to give him the desired mandate. When the votes were counted after the 1932 election, it was found that his party and its independence issue had won a mere 2 per cent of the total vote.

As recounted in Chapter I, Albizu Campos now turned to violence and had his fanatical followers begin to assassinate North Americans. Interrupted by prison sentences, Albizu's terrorism continued intermittently through the uprising of 1950 in which attempts were made on the lives of President Truman and Governor Muñoz, to March 1, 1954, when four Nationalists, in Washington, sprayed the House of Representatives with bullets in the intention of embarrassing the United States at the Tenth Inter-American Congress, which opened that day in Caracas.

A very sick man, Albizu is today serving a life sentence for inciting to murder, while Cubans and other enemies of the United States insist that he is a political prisoner who is being punished for his desire for his country's independence. Meanwhile, however, his remaining followers, the small band of Nationalists, continue to clamor for independence, though an alert police see to it that any ideas they may still harbor about committing murder are thoroughly frustrated. As a political organization, the Nationalist Party was, in 1948, replaced by the Independence Party, whose leaders seemed to think that they can obtain sovereignty by peaceful means, in a spirit of friendship, while also retaining most or all of the fiscal advantages which Puerto Rico now enjoys as a commonwealth.

THE NEW DEAL

In the 1932 election, which saw the demise of the Nationalists as a functioning political party, the Liberal Party, within which Muñoz Marín became a senator, won the plurality but lost the government just the same. It was defeated by the fact of a coalition of the Republican and Socialist parties. The Republican Party, the island's most reactionary, dominated by the feudal big landowners, came to hold the government under the rule of the ultra-conservative governor, General Blanton Winship from Georgia, who confidentially said to his friends: "I get along with the Puerto Ricans because I treat them as though they were my equals." He got along very well with his cabinet members and the island's social leaders, but he was incapable of conceiving how badly he was getting along with the island's rank and file.

POLITICAL CONFLICT IN SAN JUAN

While Puerto Rico had one of the most reactionary governments and legislatures in its history, the United States proper had one of the most liberal. Roosevelt and his New Deal were anathema to the men who ran Puerto Rico's political affairs, just as they were to the mainland Republicans. Virtually everything done on the island by the New Deal, virtually every step taken to help the starving poor, every measure adopted to reshape the economy toward the end of making it function better than formerly for the Puerto Ricans' benefit, was opposed and fought by the men who ran the island's government with the blessings of their reactionary governor.

THE RISE OF MUÑOZ MARÍN

Chapter I relates how Muñoz Marín and the little band who formed the nucleus of his new Popular Democratic Party led the people of Puerto Rico out of the depths of their despair through the revolutionary election of 1940. In every election since then, beginning in 1944, Muñoz and the party polled close to 60 per cent of the total vote, usually a little more, in 1960 a little less. Meanwhile Muñoz Marín has changed his mind about political status, has turned his back on the independence which he once advocated, has come to realize that the transformation which has attracted attention from all the world and is keenly appreciated by the Puerto Ricans themselves would have been impossible except under the American flag, as a result of cooperation between Puerto Rico and the United States.

THE FIRST PUERTO RICAN GOVERNOR

Rexford Tugwell became governor in 1942. He worked hard and well with the Puerto Rican leaders, although, as pointed out in Chapter VIII, he at times imposed his own individual will in the shaping of policies. One of his great drawbacks was that the majority in the United States Congress disliked him and all he stood for, a fact which did harm to Puerto Rico. He therefore resigned in 1946 and persuaded President Truman to appoint a Puerto Rican for at least a two-year term, as interim governor. This last was Jesús Piñero, one of the island's independent sugar planters who had long been with Muñoz Marín at least on the subject of land reform. He had, since 1944, been Puerto Rico's Resident Commissioner in the United States Congress, where he was extremely popular. The fact that now, for the first time in the island's history, a Puerto

Rican was appointed to the governship aroused great enthusiasm. If he was somewhat limited in his vision, he nevertheless worked well with Muñoz, who remained President of the Puerto Rican Senate, the island's undisputed political leader, and the shaper of its destiny. During Piñero's administration, Puerto Rico at last won the right from Congress to elect its own governor, the first to be popularly elected in a long succession of governors which had begun with Juan Ponce de León in 1508. Responsible to the people of Puerto Rico rather than to the Washington Congress and officials, this governor now also won the right to appoint his own cabinet. The control which Congress had long exercised over policies in Puerto Rican affairs, through its powers to approve or disapprove candidates for cabinet posts, had now been voluntarily relinquished.

THE END OF COLONIALISM

Muñoz Marín, campaigning against four rivals, with the island's "best" and vocal people as bitterly against him as the same people were against Roosevelt in the national scene, with every newspaper, every radio station attacking him vituperatively, won the 1948 election overwhelmingly. Within the next four years he had "solved" Puerto Rico's political problem to his own satisfaction and that of most Puerto Ricans, though not to that of the irreconcilable, reactionary upper classes. In 1950 the United States Congress passed Public Law 600, drafted in Puerto Rico, providing for an election to choose members of a constituent assembly whose task would be that of drafting a Puerto Rican constitution. If that constitution was then accepted by the Puerto Ricans in a plebiscite, and ratified by Congress, it would become the basic document under which the Puerto Ricans would thenceforth govern themselves as far as their internal affairs were concerned, while remaining citizens of the United States. Relations between Puerto Rico and the federal government were to be regulated by the so-called Federal Relations Statute, composed primarily of certain provisions of the Jones Act of 1917 which were to remain in effect.

COMMONWEALTH STATUS

On July 25, 1952, the people of Puerto Rico took their own affairs firmly into their own hands while voluntarily remaining associated with the United States as American citizens. In English, Puerto Rico is today known as a "Commonwealth." In the much more descriptive Spanish, it is an *"Estado Libre Asociado,"* or "Free, Associated State." In granting that status, the Congress voluntarily relinquished the powers to legislate specifically for Puerto Rico which it had guarded so jealously in 1900. The only federal body which can today interfere in Puerto Rican legislation is the Supreme Court, since the Puerto Ricans, as American citizens, cannot pass laws which are contrary to the United States Constitution. In fiscal matters, Puerto Rico today enjoys greater freedoms than it would have if it were a state of the Union.

The status is not yet perfect but steps are under way to improve it. Having been shaped specifically to meet Puerto Rico's needs and realities, it is unique in the world's political affairs and has for that reason been studied by a number of eminent political scientists who regard it as an example of American inventiveness, significant precisely because it came at a time when many old social and political concepts are breaking down and new ones must be created to replace them.

Markets and Politics

THE well-being and economic growth of today's
Puerto Rico rest, as it were, on a tripod composed of three specific
provisions in the island's relationship with the United States. Two
are fiscal in nature and have been in force since the passage of the
Foraker Act in 1900. They are: free trade with the United States
and exemption from contributions to the federal treasury. They provided shaky economic support until the third leg was finally
added. That was the political power, developing during the period
1941 to 1952, through which the Puerto Ricans now have control
of their own internal policies and can use their fiscal advantages for
the maximum benefit of all concerned.

THE SPANISH TRADE MONOPOLY

From their earliest days as Spanish subjects, the Puerto Ricans
were hampered by Spain's restrictive mercantilistic policies. They
were permitted to trade with nobody but the Spanish merchants
who had been granted appropriate monopolistic concessions, and
to ship their goods only in Spanish bottoms. Naturally, those regulations came to irritate the North Europeans as much as they did
the Puerto Ricans. The result was an exuberant illicit trade, a traffic
in smuggling which came to outstrip the legal commerce by far.
When the English, the French, and the Dutch were not attacking
Puerto Rico's forts, they were making inroads on the island's
commerce. The illegal trade grew by leaps and bounds after the
North Europeans had established themselves firmly in the Caribbean, had begun to cultivate sugar in such places as Haiti, Trinidad,

and Jamaica, and needed the slaves who for some time constituted the principal articles of contraband.

Writing about the eighteenth century in his engaging study, *Puerto Rico and the non-Hispanic Caribbean,* Dr. Arturo Morales Carrión says:

> Contraband was still the established mode of trade, the all-important mechanism which kept the economy going and provided new outlets for its expansion. For the islanders, in exchange for flour, wine, soap, knives, clothing and a host of other articles of which they were in great need, could offer to the contrabandist in the second half of the century not only cattle, tobacco and hides, but coffee and cotton as well. The development of coffee-planting was particularly illuminating in this regard. The plant, introduced in 1755 by Governor Felipe Ramírez de Estenós, found a most congenial soil in Puerto Rico. By 1775 it was yielding 45,049 *arrobas* (approximately 1,126,000 pounds) . . . and was in great demand by foreign smugglers who considered it the best of its kind in America and practically bought the whole harvest.

With smuggling a major business, Puerto Rico's legal export to Spain was a mere trickle, estimated at about 10,000 pesos per year. The Spanish authorities, ensconced in San Juan, simply lacked the police power which they needed, throughout the island and in the Caribbean area, for enforcing the monopoly which a generous Pope had granted them in 1493.

TRADE WITH THE UNITED STATES

Trade with the thirteen British colonies in the north seems first to have developed because San Juan's soldiers and citizens were convinced that they could not get along without flour in their diet. When the staple failed to arrive from Spain, at times because North European privateers intercepted it, the governors bought it, if illegally, from the hated Anglo-Americans who came to Puerto Rico with many other things as well and so established a growing contraband trade. After winning independence, the young United States of America tried through diplomatic channels to obtain legal trading privileges in the Spanish Caribbean possessions, while at the same time increasing its illegal trade there. Spain opened the legal door for trade in 1797, but slammed it shut again two years later. It made little difference. The fact that trade between Puerto Rico and the United States was for a brief period legal according to Spanish rulings did not at all mean that it was free. The decree of 1797 did little to stop or deter smuggling aimed at circumventing the payment of duties, port charges, and the like. When the trade door was slammed shut again by Spain in 1797, the net result was to accelerate smuggling still more.

Early in the nineteenth century, Spain's vast empire in the Americas fell to pieces, and by 1825 Puerto Rico and Cuba were the only two parts of it left as Spanish possessions. Under the stress of circumstances, the regulations governing Puerto Rico's commerce were progressively liberalized, and the island's legitimate trade rose in response. In 1813 the total value of that trade was $269,008. Three years later it had risen to $1,082,299, and by 1818 it was $2,103,498. That rise, however, was due only in part to the lifting of legal restrictions. It was augmented considerably as a result of a sudden influx of immigrants with capital from neighboring trouble-spots. In 1775, Puerto Rico's population was 70,000; by 1832 it had grown to 330,000.

TRADE AND TARIFFS

During the nineteenth century, Puerto Rico's trade with the United States increased appreciably, and the island's cane-sugar industry benefited to a marked extent. However, after beet sugar became a profitable industry in the United States and came to be protected by a tariff against tropical cane sugar with its lower cost of production, Puerto Rico's sugar industry again had a hard time. In 1870 the Puerto Rican planters clamored for free trade with the United States. Failing to get it, many of them went bankrupt, and large areas previously producing cane were perforce turned to pasture for tick-infested cattle, grown for their hides. Not until Puerto Rico came under the American flag did the island attain the free trade for which it had yearned and clamored so long.

Table 2, showing variations in Puerto Rico's external trade, tells an interesting story of political vicissitudes. The figures showing

Table 2   Puerto Rico's External Trade—Exports Plus Imports

Year	Total Trade	Trade with United States	U.S. Share of Total	Per Capita Total	U.S.
1900-01	$ 17,492,103	$ 12,536,696	72%	$ 18	$ 14
1910-11	$ 78,705,374	$ 69,437,367	88%	$ 70	$ 62
1920-21	$ 217,758,278	$ 200,462,676	92%	$167	$154
1930-31	$ 174,838,337	$ 162,895,164	92%	$113	$105
1941-42 *	$ 258,608,609	$ 245,319,884	95%	$137	$131
1950-51	$ 708,777,480	$ 654,763,203	93%	$311	$297
1958-59	$1,311,957,662	$1,153,650,674	89%	$575	$500

* Figures for 1940-41 not available.

the share of the total trade going to the United States are striking. Already 72 per cent when Puerto Rico first became a colony of the United States, this share rose sharply to 95 per cent during the war year 1941-42, when the island was more or less cut off from the rest of the world, and declined to 89 per cent in 1958-59, in part as a result of the Puerto Ricans' own efforts to broaden their commercial contacts and expand their trade base.

ABSENTEE CONTROL

The dramatic rise in trade between 1901 and 1921, from $17 million to $218 million, was less healthful for Puerto Rico than statistics alone would indicate. To a large extent it reflected the investments of American corporate capital in the island's economy, which, in an exploitative, monopolistic manner, exported a large share of the profits together with the products, controlled much of Puerto Rico's political life, and created sweatshop economic conditions. Even today, the large trade with the United States is not entirely healthful. As shown in Chapter VII, a considerable part of it can be traced to the importation into Puerto Rico of millions of dollars worth of foodstuffs which the Puerto Ricans may some day again be able to produce themselves.

The decline in trade between 1921 and 1931, 20 per cent, going hand in hand with an even greater (21 per cent) increase in population, reflects the sufferings of the depression period which began in 1929. During the next four years, between 1931 and 1935, the total trade slipped another 25 per cent, while the population grew by some 12 per cent.

TRADE AND POLITICAL EMANCIPATION

By 1942, in part because of recovery from the world depression, the trade had again risen appreciably, to a figure somewhat higher than that of 1921, though the *per capita* trade was still lower by $30 than it had been two decades earlier. The rise in trade after 1942 is truly startling and can be traced primarily to internal political developments. The Puerto Ricans had by now attained the political power to curb the monopolistic mainland sugar corporations, which had always resisted a general, integrated economic development. They had broadened their industrial and economic base immeasurably. They had increased their gross product from $287 million in 1940 to $1,789 million in 1961, their per capita average annual income during the same period, from $121 to $621. The shipping business boomed as a result.

BROADENED PHILOSOPHY OF DEVELOPMENT

As shown in Chapter VIII, moreover, in 1948 the Puerto Ricans changed their basic policy for industrialization from a local matter geared to local capital, raw materials, and markets, to a national movement, tapping the vast resources in capital, raw materials, and purchasing power of the United States. The increase in trade with the United States between 1951 and 1959 from $655 million to $1,154 million reflects not only a dramatic growth in industrialization, but also the change in policy under which a large number of factories now have to rely on ocean shipping, not only for access to their markets but also for their raw materials.

THE BALANCE OF PAYMENTS

By 1959 Puerto Rico had risen to sixth place among the world's purchasers of American goods, being topped only by Canada, the United Kingdom, Japan, Germany, and Venezuela. Moreover, the island's *per capita* purchases of American goods, $290 in 1959, were the world's highest. During 1958-59, the island's total imports were $809 million, while exports came to $503 million. However, the indicated imbalance of trade was and is today only apparent. Compensating factors which militate for a healthy trade picture include:

(1) Federal expenditures in Puerto Rico for the armed forces, the Post Office, and the like;

(2) United States grants-in-aid for road construction, schools, health, agriculture, and the like, which in 1960 totaled almost $30 million;

(3) Remission to Puerto Rico of customs duties, excise taxes, etc., amounting to another $30 million;

(4) Remittances sent back to the island by Puerto Ricans living in the United States; and, finally,

(5) The fact that many of Puerto Rico's imports, during the present period of rapid economic growth, consist of such capital goods as machinery, purchased for the purpose of creating new wealth.

THE HIGH COST OF LIVING

In the face of such massive economic progress, surprise is often expressed over the fact that Puerto Rico's wages, while rising steadily as a result of governmental and union efforts, are still considerably lower than are those on the mainland while the cost of living, despite constant governmental efforts to keep it down, remains considerably higher except for the lowest income groups, whose needs remain lower than do those of corresponding groups in the north. The reasons for these phenomena are many and varied. Among them may be counted a remaining number of greedy, profiteering merchants whose influences on the cost of living are now, to some extent, being offset by the inauguration of a large number of chain stores, supermarkets, and shopping centers. The ever-present, avid speculators in real estate, whom nobody has to date been able to curb[1] but whose bubble of prosperity seems inexorably headed for bursting, have also, to date, contributed to the high cost of living. Beyond such factors, however, the fact remains that, as pointed out in Chapter III, life on an island, depending on ocean shipping for the means of subsistence, tends to be relatively expensive. The knotty problem of freight rates is always uppermost in the minds of both government and business. While inclusion within the American tariff barrier, resulting in duty-free trade with the United States, is an undeniable, essential boon for Puerto Rico, every increase in shipping rates obviously makes that trade less "free."

THE PROBLEM OF FREIGHT RATES

The same Foraker Act of 1900 which gave Puerto Rico free trade with the United States also included the island within the terms of the Coastwise Shipping Laws, under which cargoes shipped between United States ports must be carried in American steamers, whose operating costs and resulting freight rates are the world's highest. American ships operating in foreign trade today enjoy federal subsidies, aimed at keeping the merchant marine afloat through compensation for the cost-differentials between foreign and domestic operations. American ships engaged in the "coastwise" trade, exclusively between United States ports, are given no such subsidies and must meet their operating costs entirely through freight charges. The higher their costs, they argue before the Federal Maritime Commission in Washington, the higher their rates must obviously be. Between March 14, 1946, and January 15, 1958, five such increases became effective in the Puerto Rican trade. Today the rates in that trade are more than twice as high as they were at the end of World War II, while rates from West Coast ports have risen by almost 80 per cent since 1951.

[1] Under a law passed in 1962, the government is now actively combatting the speculators by going into the land business itself.

PUERTO RICO'S CLAIMS

Every request for an increase is, of course, fought bitterly (so far without success) by the Puerto Rican government, which argues that the requests are exorbitant and that every increase in rates must be paid by every resident of Puerto Rico, through lower wages, higher costs of living, and increases in manufacturing costs, especially where raw materials must be imported and finished products exported by sea.

The following quotation from the government report, "Puerto Rico's Problems with the United States Maritime Laws," is revealing. "The accounts of the Maritime Administration show operating differential subsidies of $152.7 million for 1959. This amounts to $0.89 per capita for the population of the United States. . . . In contrast the burden of $10 million[2] on the Puerto Rican people . . . amounted to $4.28 per capita. . . . However, average personal income in Puerto Rico in 1959 was only $511 against $2,165 in the continental United States."

In the same pamphlet, the Puerto Rican government suggests rather mildly that Washington might open shipping between Puerto Rico and the continental United States to unrestricted competition from foreign operators. Early in 1961, Puerto Rico joined with Hawaii and Alaska, which have similar problems, in requesting that ships plying between their ports and the mainland be granted the federal subsidies which are given to American vessels in foreign trade.

TECHNICAL IMPROVEMENTS

While the argument between the government and most of the steamship companies goes on, with some companies claiming that they lose millions of dollars in the Puerto Rican trade, relief is also sought through technological improvements. The old-fashioned stevedoring is a slow and costly method of handling cargoes in the ports. Every hour during which a ship is unnecessarily tied up at a

---

[2] Estimated as the annual difference in operating costs between United States ships and potential foreign ships in the Puerto Rican trade.

pier, every increase in the wages of dock workers, increases the cost of operation and so, eventually, the freight rates charged.

Some of the companies are of course also doing what they can to lower operating costs, as for example by turning to various types of "container" shipments in which cargoes are packed in large metal containers or trailers which can be handled by cranes and thereby reduce the expense of loading by stevedores. Outstandingly successful in that field is the so-called "Sea-Land Service" which has been in Puerto Rican operations since 1958. Ships specially designed for the purpose carry cargoes exclusively in trailer-sized containers which can not only be lifted bodily at the ports onto the waiting trailer-chassis, also specially designed for the purpose, but can also be loaded on railroad freight cars for transportation, for instance, between Chicago and New York. The service reduces the costs of transportation by reducing the costs of loading and land transportation. Within such trends, the possibility is even now being discussed of Puerto Rico, at some future date, becoming an entrepot between New York and California. At certain times of the year, when cargoes from New York to Puerto Rico are relatively light, steamers can fill them out by carrying a number of trailers destined for the West Coast, which can be left in San Juan to be picked up later by California-bound vessels.

THE EVOLUTION OF PORTS

Such new methods of handling freight call for changes in port facilities. Goods handled the old-fashioned way require closed storage space at the ports. Goods shipped in containers or trailers require open areas. Every change in handling freight calls for a corresponding change in Puerto Rico's piers.

The problem of sugar was mentioned in Chapter II but should be discussed somewhat more fully. During the 1930's, Puerto Rico had 20 active seaports, 17 of which were devoted exclusively to shipping sugar. Most of the latter had no pier facilities; the sugar, packed in jute bags, was lightered to the anchored steamers. When lighterage became obsolete through being relatively too expensive, the island's sugar crop was shipped, still in bags, through a few ports which had pier facilities. Eventually, too, that system of shipping became uneconomical. Today the entire sugar crop is shipped unbagged, in bulk, through four specially constructed piers and is handled almost entirely by machinery at the mill as well as the port. The new system, while badly needed to keep Puerto Rico's sugar industry afloat in the face of stiff competition from other locales, is hard on the stevedores. By the same token it creates political problems; a stevedore who loses his work is apt to turn into an enemy of the ruling party. The government has negotiated a contract under which the sugar shippers using the new bulk-system of shipping pay a bonus to the stevedores for a certain period of time, after which the government hopes to have created new sources of employment for them.

Gasoline, which until a few years ago came in as such to a number of ports for internal distribution by tank-trucks, now enters in the form of crude oil, delivered over special piers to two refineries which fill all of Puerto Rico's needs for vehicle fuel. Rice and flour, until very recent times, came to Puerto Rico from the mainland in bags, barrels, and retail packages. Today they come in bulk, the rice unpolished, the flour in the form of grain, to be processed in specially built plants in San Juan harbor, whose byproducts, together with sugar's molasses, have become important cattle feeds. But, again, the stevedores suffer.

THE POSSIBILITY OF A MERCHANT MARINE

Today there is much talk about the possibility of establishing a Puerto Rican merchant marine which could be operated at least for "yardstick" purposes, be the proposed fleet owned publicly, privately, or in a combination of the two. The example and experiences of another island society tend to encourage such a step. In 1913, with shipping problems somewhat similar to today's Puerto Rico but with a population of fewer than 150,000, Iceland created its own merchant fleet through the sale of stock to virtually its entire population as well as to thousands of "West Icelanders" living in America. The Icelandic shipping company has since then been an outstanding success. On the other hand, it is not at all certain that the Commonwealth government would be able to operate a shipping line more economically than do the present private own-ers. As pointed out in Chapter VIII, the government's operation of factories during the early stages of industrialization resulted largely in financial losses. Even today, while the government is outstand-ingly successful in several such activities as the generation and distribution of electric power, it has also suffered a number of costly and embarrassing failures in other branches of economic endeavor. Because of such experiences, an alternate scheme is now being con-sidered under which at least one steamship company, with mini-mum profits guaranteed, may agree to being declared a public util-ity, its operations, rates, and the like being regulated by the Public Service Commission.

AIR SERVICE

All the steamers in the Puerto Rican trade (except of course the cruise ships which visit the island in increasing numbers) are freight ships, though some of them have accommodations for twelve passengers each. The operators claim that they cannot, without federal subsidies, afford to run passenger ships to Puerto Rico. The island must therefore depend almost exclusively on air transport for its passenger services. The growth of air transporta-tion has been remarkable. The number of plane passengers, coming and going, rose from 316,736 in 1950 to 1,416,158 ten years later. During the same period, air freight and express soared from 10,592 tons to 25,280. However, even in that field the Puerto Ricans find it difficult to keep abreast of the world. San Juan's beautiful Interna-tional Airport, the island's principal port of entry for passengers, was opened in 1955, designed to meet all needs until 1975. By 1960, ;o phenomenal was the increase in traffic, it was already too small in all its facilities and had to be enlarged in a hurry.

TODAY'S POLITICAL PROBLEM

We have attempted to show that every economic advance in Puerto Rico was accompanied, or caused by, a political change. Con-versely, every future political change will inevitably find its counter-part in a corresponding economic change. To a far too great extent,

Puerto Rico's modern political debate still centers on the question of relations with the United States. A considerable proportion of Puerto Ricans still insist that the island's present status cannot be permanent and that it must in the end give way to either independence or statehood. While their claim that commonwealth status cannot be permanent is unproved and probably incorrect, it is still interesting to note that sovereign independence would deprive Puerto Rico of one leg of its progress-supporting tripod, namely free trade with the United States, while statehood would deprive it of one of the others, exemption from contributions to the federal treasury. The case against statehood will be dealt with later; a few words about Puerto Rico's possible independence will suffice here.

THE CASE AGAINST INDEPENDENCE

In 1959, Puerto Rico shipped $104 million worth of sugar products to the United States. It is well known that the industry would collapse if, as a republic, Puerto Rico had to pay duty on such exports. Going down the line, one finds that during that same year, to mention only two specific examples, the island's exports of electrical machinery and apparatus to the United States, virtually all of them made from imported raw materials, totaled $47 million, while cotton manufactures shipped to the States totaled $43 million. Like sugar, those industries could not survive the imposition of a tariff. The point is that under independence much of Puerto Rico's agricultural and industrial effort would inevitably collapse, while the island would also lose the benefit of United States grants-in-aid and would have to assume the burden of maintaining its own diplomatic staff as well as its own armed forces. It is true that an independent Puerto Rico could reduce its shipping costs by getting out from under the Coastwise Shipping Laws and so being able to use foreign steamers. However, since the hypothetical republic, its economy seriously impaired, would have much less to ship than the commonwealth has today, the advantage of lower rates would be of little avail.[3]

[3] The present advocates of independence seem to believe that the island can attain sovereignty while retaining most or all financial advantages of its present relations with the United States.

VII   *The Agricultural Base*

"T HE Spanish settler in Puerto Richo," writes Morales Carrión, "did not come primarily as a tiller of the soil. As elsewhere in the Indies, he was a crown officer, a trader, a founder of towns. He was impatient, restless, eager for fame and wealth. . . . A precursor of the modern *entrepreneur,* he organized the early economic enterprises through the utilization of cheap available labor. It was natural for him to turn to mining as the most promising short cut to wealth and glory."

The earliest settlers taught Indians to mine their gold and grow their foods, but the gold proved scarce and the Indians made a poor labor force. Many died and more withdrew into the wild, mountainous interior where they came eventually to be exterminated in the cultural sense but absorbed in the biological. In some interior regions today, thousands of the so-called *jíbaros,* the rural peasantry, cheerful, gentle, proud, and hospitable, show unmistakable Indian traits.

The shortage of labor plagued the colonists from the beginning and became doubly acute when the realization arose, very shortly after Ponce de León's arrival in 1508, that Puerto Rico's economy would have to shift from a mining base to one of agriculture. As Europe developed a fast-mounting craving for sugar, the West Indies developed a corresponding craving for slaves to produce it. A few of the first settlers, in Puerto Rico, Hispaniola, and Cuba, had brought Negro slaves with them to help with the household chores. Their fame for hardihood and successful adjustment to the climate soared with the settlers' yearning for more such slaves.

"So well did the Negroes adjust themselves to Española," wrote an early chronicler, "that people used to say that only hanging could

kill a Negro, for no one had seen them die a natural death." African men and women became valuable items of commerce throughout the West Indies as early as 1518. The Crown granted the privi-
lege of trading in them to certain monopolistic individuals or
groups, and came eventually and at times to charge export taxes
and import duties on them, which naturally accelerated the contraband commerce in human souls. However they were brought, legally or illegally, Negroes came to Puerto Rico's coastal plains to till
the soil and harvest sugar cane. They introduced African strains of
music, African ceremonials, African witch-doctor medicine, and a
new infusion of blood for the island's ethnic melting pot.

THE RISE OF SUGAR

However, the development of a sugar economy required more
than land and slaves. Sugar is an industrial, capitalist crop, requiring investment in mills. Again and again the Crown was asked
not only to provide slaves, but also to set up government-owned
mills where people could have their cane ground for fees, or to provide credit to progressive individuals who wanted to build their
own mills. The Spanish government was slow to respond, a fact
which intensified the settlers' eagerness to leave Puerto Rico and
move to Peru. It became apparent that the only way to prevent the
island's depopulation was through the development of a sugar industry.

From Spain's point of view sugar had the advantage, in addition
to being a profitable crop, of being more amenable to control than
other crops, more easily kept out of the contraband trade and held
in legal channels within the Spanish trade monopoly. The advantage was of course relative; actually, as Puerto Rico's rural population increased and became increasingly disdainful of royal com-
mands originating in Spain and channeled to Puerto Rico via the
audiencia in Hispaniola, no item of commerce could be kept out of
the smugglers' hands. The Portuguese, for instance, expert contra-
bandists and often acting with the connivance of the local Spanish
authorities, early began to bring in slaves without securing licenses,
registering their cargoes in Seville, or paying duties. Since cash was

scarce in Puerto Rico, they exchanged their cargoes for sugar and hides.

SUGAR AND LATIFUNDIA

Sugar's demand for the investment of capital in mills by the same token also tends to promote *latifundia,* or concentration of land in large estates. The man who invests in a mill wants to control plenty of land around it to guarantee its steady, profitable operation. Very early in Puerto Rico's history, therefore, the flat lands on the coastal plains, the island's best agricultural areas, came to be concentrated in large holdings, owned by relatively few people. The latecomers, those who arrived during and after the seventeenth century, encroached on the interior where they could obtain crown lands at relatively low cost. There, after 1755, they produced coffee in the western mountains, tobacco and diversified crops in the eastern. They also produced food for the cities, but were again handicapped by royal decrees. For instance, they were not permitted, lest they develop seafaring techniques of their own, to transport their crops by sea along the coasts; they had to bring them to town overland. Since the trails were tortuous, the country-people often preferred to sell their crops to obliging smugglers, thereby leaving the cities, and especially San Juan, recurringly short of food. Ginger proved to be an excellent item of illicit trade, greatly in demand by the smugglers. An order therefore went out from the authorities to stop growing it, but there is no indication that the order was obeyed.

AGRICULTURAL PATTERN

The agricultural pattern that had developed toward the end of the Spanish regime was one of cash-export crops, namely sugar, coffee, and tobacco (citrus fruits were added early during the American regime), produced on large estates by and for the small class of dominating land-owners, while the masses of the poor worked for miserable, peonage wages or eked bare existences out of barren, sloping soils.

Absentee ownership of the most productive lands began to arise early during the nineteenth century, when Spain rescinded not only the trade monopoly which had been on the statute books for three centuries, but also the earlier ban on foreign settlers and foreign enterprise in Puerto Rico. Such absentee ownership was intensified after the onset of United States control, appearing largely in sugar and to a lesser extent in tobacco and citrus fruits. Coffee was and remains a Puerto Rican crop, produced by Puerto Ricans, on land owned by Puerto Ricans, and until recently worked by miserable Puerto Rican peons existing in animal-like fashion. Until early in the twentieth century, however, Puerto Rican coffee remained a prized crop, greatly in demand for its quality in Europe and even in Cuba. Its subsequent decline resulted from a combination of causes, including several devastating hurricanes, shipping interruptions during World War I, general changes in the world's coffee market, and changes in the tariff situation.

THE CASE OF COFFEE

Free trade with the United States benefited Puerto Rican producers of sugar and tobacco because their foreign competitors had to pay duty on importing those goods. However, there was and is no duty on coffee.[1] In former days, Puerto Rican coffee enjoyed tariff protection from Spain, whence it was distributed throughout Europe, while duty had to be paid on other coffees. That advantage was lost to the island's coffee growers when they came under the American flag.

Moreover, many of Puerto Rico's coffee *fincas* are today, in part because of conservatism, among the world's least efficient, producing an average of 200 pounds per acre, while Hawaii, at times and in places, produces 2,000. Even after allowances have been made for widespread efforts at tax evasion which undoubtedly depress the figures reported by a number of growers, even when one brings the 200 pounds up to a more probable 500, Puerto Rican coffee culture is still in bad shape. It could not and cannot compete in the

[1] While no duty is charged on foreign coffee imported into the United States proper, such duty has in recent years been levied on coffee imported into Puerto Rico.

United States market with coffees imported from elsewhere and is today produced, against stiff competition from advertised American brands, almost exclusively for the Puerto Rican market. Coffee is today Puerto Rico's most stricken crop. The coffee regions are the island's most fertile seed-beds for migrants to New York and elsewhere on the mainland. The exodus intensifies the labor problem and increases the burdens of the large producers.

THE QUEST FOR SOLUTIONS

The Commonwealth's Department of Agriculture is today carrying on an energetic campaign, introducing new, quick-maturing varieties, cultivated intensively by modern means and requiring no shade trees as Puerto Rican coffee does today. But the going is hard. While the yield on the new plantings is considerably greater than on the old, the costs involved are considerable. The elimination of shade trees calls for much more fertilization and weeding than were needed for coffee grown by the long-established methods. This, to be done efficiently by mechanical means, requires reasonably flat land, but most Puerto Rican coffee is today grown on steep slopes. Free fertilizers supplied by the government, plus price supports, are insufficient to permit the payment of wages much above 35 cents per hour. The migrant Puerto Rican laborer who has become accustomed to receiving $1.00 per hour in New Jersey does not take kindly to the lower figure.

While there are some who maintain that a good living can still be made on family-sized *fincas* where children are used as cheap labor, the general trend is in the direction of making it a crop produced by the well-to-do who have the capital required for the change-over to modern methods. Meanwhile the government remains sentimental about coffee as a typical Puerto Rican crop, while taking some steps toward diversification.

Some of the coffee lands which have been abandoned in recent decades are now being planted to pasture grasses and put to producing cattle. At least one owner of a coffee plantation has converted two-thirds of his land to pasture on which he is now producing beef cattle. Since cattle require horses, and since the magnificent mountain scenery is a fine tourist attraction, the man has now branched out into a "guest-plantation" business. Tourists, dude-ranching, and the production of meat now keep his field hands busy and help to support the coffee production, itself exploitable as a tourist attraction, on the 250 acres he has reserved for that crop.

THE NEED FOR INTEGRATED REGIONAL PLANNING

Whatever may or may not happen to save Puerto Rico's coffee industry, it is obvious that it can best be saved, not by any one drastic step or technical program, but through the social-economic diversification which is increasingly a hallmark of modern Puerto Rico. It will not be coffee alone which is saved; it will be a region, through being developed for everything it has to offer by way of recreation, crops new to it, and new social systems, possibly including new systems of land tenure.

CHANGES IN LAND TENURE

THE FIVE-HUNDRED ACRE LAW

Puerto Rico's first organic act under the United States, the Foraker Act of 1900, included a provision known as the "Five-Hundred Acre Law," making it illegal for a corporation to own or control more than 500 acres of land. Senator Foraker insisted that he had written the provision into his act in order to protect the island from the inroads of large corporations. There is reason to believe, however, that he did it at the request of the farm lobby, which wanted to protect its continental beet sugar against the rise of a significant cane sugar industry in America's new tropical colony. Whatever the reasons for the law, it had no teeth, provided no penalties for non-observance. Immediately after the onset of United States rule, it began to be ignored with a vengeance. Four powerful mainland corporations came to Puerto Rico and obtained land on the fertile coastal plains through purchase, lease, or the foreclosure of mortgages. They built modern mills and created economic conditions conducive to the creation of modern seaports, highways, and a railroad running around the island, primarily for the transportation of cane.[2] The largest of the "Big Four," the Eastern Puerto Rico Sugar Co., by 1940 managed a plantation of 54,700 acres, of which only 20,900 were planted to cane; the rest were held in reserve or used for pasturing oxen while landless Puerto Ricans looked on.

SUGAR AND ABSENTEE PRODUCTION

The production and export of sugar soared phenomenally. By 1912 it had reached almost 400,000 tons, or ten times as much as it had been during the low year 1898-99. In 1934 sugar production reached the all-time high of 1,114,000 tons, albeit for sale in the low-price depression market. The nature of Puerto Rico's one-crop, absentee-dominated economy, typical of so many Latin American societies, may be judged from the fact that in that year sugar accounted for 62 per cent of the total dollar value ($87 million) of Puerto Rico's exports, while in turn some 60 per cent of the sugar shipments were exported, together with the profits thereon, by the four powerful United States corporations, leaving little behind but starvation wages and extremely low taxes.

After 1934, through the Costigan-Jones Act, the island's total sugar production was curtailed to a quota, the growers being paid bonuses for the sugar not produced though the workers who lost their jobs received nothing and so came to swell all the more the mounting federal relief rolls. The quota, originally 802,848 tons, has by now (1961) been raised to 1,270,865 tons. The industry, on the other hand, has in recent years been unable to meet its quota. Rising production costs, floods and other phenomena, and occasional shortages of labor in certain areas account in part for the shortages. A contributing factor is that the cane's sugar content has decreased because the industry, faced with economic problems, has failed to replant its cane every five years, as it should.

THE REVOLUTION AND LAND TENURE

Under existing federal laws, most of the sugar shipped to the United States must be in crude form, to be refined on the mainland.

[2] Early during the 1950's, the railroad went out of business. It was replaced by trucks, which, while more economical for hauling purposes, now create serious problems of road congestion at harvest time.

Of the quota total, only 148,306 tons may be shipped in refined form, while another 120,000 tons may be refined for local use.
Enacted during the 1930's to protect mainland refiners against undue competition from the island, the restriction on local refining
is widely resented as a remnant of colonialism.

The revolutionary election of 1940 broke the sugar industry's
political power and gave it to the island's voters. Like virtually
every revolution of modern times, Puerto Rico's was from the first
deeply concerned with land-tenure. The new government invoked
the federal "Five-Hundred Acre Law" and set out, as funds became
available, to expropriate lands held by corporations in excess of the
legal limit. It so happened that these were primarily the absentee
concerns. Local land-owning corporations were and are largely
family affairs which can easily be split up into legal units con-
trolling 500 acres or less, while being operated just as before. The
result is that there is still too much concentration of land in large
estates to suit the island's agricultural planners. One of several reasons why agricultural development has lagged behind industrial is
that nearly 50 per cent of all the land in farms (1,844,886 acres) is
still concentrated in a mere 3 per cent of the total number (53,515)
of farms.

GOVERNMENT COMPETITION

Having acquired land through expropriation as well as through
such measures as swamp drainage, the government now went into
the business of producing sugar cane while the large corporations
remained in the manufacturing business of grinding it. A total of
63 government "proportional profit farms," so-called because the
profits from them are returned to the workers in proportion to
wages earned, now harvest sugar from a total of 29,000 acres comprising about 10 per cent of the total land in sugar. In addition the
government has purchased two mills of its own and operates them
primarily for "yardstick" purposes to gauge relations between
growers and grinders. Moreover, organized with federal help during the depression days, two highly successful cooperatives of cane
growers now own and operate their own mills.

The Puerto Rican techniques of handling the absentee sugar companies, by first curbing their political power, then forcing them through higher wages and increased taxation to contribute more than formerly to the economy, and finally going into business in competition with them, have in more recent years been applied by Costa Rica in the field of bananas, and by Venezuela in that of oil. Puerto Rico's Governor Muñoz Marín, Costa Rica's former President and outstanding political philosopher, Dr. José Figueres, and Venezuela's present President, Rómulo Betancourt, have for years been close personal friends and are today regarded by many as a triumvirate of outstanding leaders in the current, democratic "Alliance for Progress" trends.

USES OF GOVERNMENT LANDS

Some of the land acquired by the government and not needed for the production of sugar is divided into family-sized farms and sold to individuals against long-term payments. Some, especially on the proportional profit farms, is divided into plots of half an acre or so to which eligible workers and others obtain lifelong usufruct rights gratis, the government retaining title in order to prevent a new wave of real-estate speculation. It was in those settlements, each with its cooperative store, credit union, church, school, and playing field, that the famous $400 rural houses were developed. These are attractive concrete homes, vermin-proof, hurricane-proof, and fire-proof, in the construction of which the people donate their labor while the government furnishes materials at cost and supervision gratis. The owner (who has title to the home and can pass it on to his heirs, although he doesn't own the land,) pays $15.00 down and the rest in interest-free installments of some $3.00 per month.

THE "VICIOUS CIRCLE"

Government-owned land is also used for the purpose of diversifying agriculture. For instance, it had long been realized that pineapples are an excellent crop for Puerto Rico, bringing approximately the same per-acre return as sugar and not competing with sugar for the same land. However, it was necessary for economic

health that the crop be industrialized through the construction of
a modern cannery which would play the same role vis-à-vis pineapple farmers that the sugar mills play for the cane growers. The
same "vicious circle" which constantly plagues emerging societies
in many branches of their economies seemed to stand in the way
of such a plant. Because there was no cannery, farmers were not
producing pineapples. Because farmers were not producing pineapples, private capital was unwilling to build a cannery without
acquiring an accompanying plantation larger than the law allowed.
The government therefore introduced the proper types of pineapples, propagated them on government lands, eventually built the
world's largest pineapple cannery, distributed cuttings to nearby
farmers, and went into the business of producing and canning pineapples while a private firm tended to the distribution in the United
States on a contract basis.

That general method of using a bit of state socialism to break the
"vicious circle" and so encourage capitalist expansion was also used
in the case of a new, government-built slaughterhouse, and with outstanding success in the tourist industry, where the government had
to take the plunge and build what is today the world's most profitable hotel, the Caribe Hilton, owned by the government and operated by the Hilton Company. Before 1950, the tourists were not
coming to Puerto Rico because there were no good hotels, while
private enterprise refused to build such hotels because the tourists
weren't coming. Today the tourist industry is booming. New lux-
ury hotels have been built and continue to be built, many in part
with government money. Guest houses spring up, and during the
year 1960-61 it was estimated that 385,000 visitors spent a total of
$55 million in Puerto Rico.

AGRICULTURE AND INDUSTRY

TOBACCO

The need for rationalizing agriculture through industrialization
is fully realized by the Economic Development Administration,

which, in its program for attracting capital and promoting manufacturing, regards industries to process agricultural products as being near the top in its list of preferences. So, for instance, the Consolidated Cigar Corporation, in 1952, opened the world's largest cigar factory in Caguas and today operates three plants in Puerto Rico. Making cigars by hand had long been an established Puerto Rican industry, but the process had been slow and working conditions were not of the best. In fact, many of the island's labor leaders had their starts as "readers" in such factories, whose job it was to lull the workers into contentment by reading newspapers to them, but who often managed to arouse them instead by exhorting them to action in the same sing-song tones with which they gave the news. There are still a number of small factories in Puerto Rico where cigars are made by hand, but their labor relations are regulated by the government, while the efficient modern plants, whose wages are good and labor relations excellent, are primarily responsible for the fact that Puerto Rico's export of cigars rose from $140,000 in 1955 to nearly $12 million in 1959.

DAIRY FARMING

Rising standards of living and the government's tireless distribution of low-cost electric energy to all parts of rural and urban Puerto Rico, which in turn permits the wide distribution of refrigerators, have lifted the business of producing fresh milk to second place, lagging behind only sugar in agricultural production. Inefficient and over-competitive distribution, however, results in much waste. In Denmark, where the cooperative movement has streamlined the distribution and conversion of milk into such things as cheese and butter, 10 good cows constitute an adequate economic unit; in Puerto Rico, where the organization and effective operation of producers' dairy cooperatives are impeded by the rich farmers' adamant demand for a high unit price for milk, much milk goes to waste during certain seasons of the year, while it requires about 100 cows to form an economic unit of minimal adequacy.

Notable among the government's efforts, too, is the Lajas Valley project in the southeast part of the island, where the generation of hydroelectricity is integrated with the irrigation of farmlands and the distribution of safe water to a number of towns and large rural areas. But there, too, the prevailing distribution of land resulting from long-established tenure patterns tends to concentrate the economic benefits into the hands of very few farmers.

AGRICULTURAL PLANNING

Several comprehensive agricultural "plans" have been drafted since 1950, of which Nathan Koenig's, mentioned above, is one, and that of Scott Keyes (as yet not released), is another. They are valuable documents which indicate desirable agricultural policies but cannot be carried out *in toto* because of uneven land-distribution, antiquated practices and viewpoints, and every farmer's need for making an immediate living. The Keyes plan, for instance, is primarily a proposal for rural zoning under which certain areas should (at least in theory) be planted only to certain crops, while some 25 per cent of all the island's land is, because of its steep slopes, recommended exclusively for trees and tree crops. Rural zoning, however, poses difficult problems. The government cannot, with any authority, tell a farmer what to plant and what not to plant; it cannot, without at least providing him with a crop which is better from both an agricultural and a market point of view, insist that he stop producing something which ruins the land.

MAINLAND COMPETITION

While much progress has been made, the fact remains that Puerto Rico still imports $162 million worth of edible animal and vegetable products annually and that a good many of those millions should go to Puerto Rican farmers. In fact, recent decades have seen a massive rise in the importation of foods, caused in part by the local farmers' inability to compete with the highly organized and streamlined foodstuffs industry in the mainland United States, in part by changing food habits, and in part by the dramatic increase of local purchasing power.

A study of eleven foods (rice, beans, meats and meat-products, processed milk, lard, flour, codfish, eggs, coffee, corn, and potatoes) tells a revealing story. During the depression year 1934, the total importation of those commodities amounted to $14,984,000, or $8.60 per capita. By 1941 they had risen to $19,824,000, or $10.30 per capita. In 1956, despite strides in agricultural development, the imports of those items totalled $99,201,000, or $43.30 per capita. At the turn of the century, the island was virtually self-sufficient in rice, though farmers were rapidly abandoning its production as being uneconomic in the face of competition from North Carolina and California. In 1934 Puerto Rico imported $6,539,000 worth, a figure which rose to nearly $30 million by 1960.

The government's construction of a modern slaughterhouse, going hand in hand with a program to distribute seeds for pasture grasses as well as beef-cattle, mentioned above, came about as a result of similar trends in meat and meat products. Their importation, $2,588,000 in 1934, had risen to $3,338,000 in 1941, $25,847,000 in 1956, and today exceeds $32 million.

The desired local production of other foods now imported largely from the United States is far less a matter of improving agricultural techniques and teaching them to local farmers than it is one of streamlining distribution to a point where Puerto Rican farmers can compete with those in the industrialized United States and can obtain the credit they need for improving their agricultural methods. The many new supermarkets, which have become phenomenally successful since their first establishment in 1956, are becoming important outlets for the products of those farmers who have learned the arts of grading and packaging and can so stagger their crops that they don't come on the market all at once. Nevertheless, the supermarkets must still import the bulk of even their fruits and fresh vegetables from the mainland, to say nothing of bread, cheeses, and eggs. Quite possibly, Puerto Rico can not hope ever to be self-sufficient in foods but there is still room for great improvement in that respect. Continued efforts to promote a healthy canning industry, to strengthen the cooperative movement in all its varied aspects, to ease farm credit, to train farmers in better production methods, to improve the distribution of foods on the island and increase their export—such and many other steps, integrated each with all the others, are required to bring Puerto Rican agriculture to its optimum effectiveness.

THE COMPLEXITIES
OF AGRICULTURAL IMPROVEMENT

Puerto Rico again teaches the lesson that the improvement of a society's agriculture requires far more than the technical improvement of its farming methods. To a far greater degree it requires drastic changes in the complex society itself, its economic life, its political orientations, its merchandising and distribution system, its transportation, internal and external, its food habits, its credit structure, and many other things. While such lessons were being learned, however, Puerto Rico's net income from agriculture rose from $70 million in 1940 to $200 million in 1961.

VIII *The Battle for Employment*

"You can't plan under capitalism, and you certainly can't plan in and for a helpless colony of the world's greatest capitalist nation." The pessimism of the young university teachers who, during the 1930's, tried to come to grips with their society's problems was understandable. As stated in Chapter III, their efforts were more or less nullified by three massive facts, namely:

(1) employed by the federal government instead of forming an integral part of the Puerto Rican, they lacked the power and political machinery for seeing their plans translated into programs of action;

(2) the government then in power in Puerto Rico was in any event so reactionary that no drastic programs to remedy existing distress could be expected from it; and

(3) business interests in the mainland United States did all they could, in order to retain their own lucrative but depression-shrunk markets in Puerto Rico, to impede local Puerto Rican economic development. Nevertheless, the depression planners did invaluable work in studying and pinpointing their society's problems and in suggesting solutions. They had no way of knowing that within a few brief years both the local scene and the world scene would change so drastically that they would be able to roll up their sleeves and pick up the tasks which they had been more or less forced to abandon in 1936.

DUAL REVOLUTION

Politically, the revolutionary election of 1940 amounted not only to an assault on colonialism under which the Puerto Ricans began to take into their own hands the powers formerly wielded by their rulers in Washington. It was also an internal revolt on the part of the island's liberal and progressive elements against the conservative, vested interests which had previously dominated Puerto Rico's government. One may doubt, however, whether that revolution could have succeeded as brilliantly as it did, had it not been an early, integral part of the world revolution, largely economic, which has by now called for the Alliance for Progress and "aid" programs throughout the former colonial world outside of the communist sphere.

The basic principle under which the depression spelled the end of colonialism everywhere, the fact that capitalism's production had so outstripped its purchasing power that new customers must be created in a hurry out of colonialism's exploited subjects, was widely recognized in general but narrowly accepted by individual enterprises. Their officials gave lip service to the principle, but continued, perforce, to safeguard their own interests by such practices as dumping. World War II changed that situation drastically.

While war shortages of goods, machinery, and at times even foods, created serious problems, they were by the same token impelling incentives for accelerated local production. In that, Puerto Rico was of course not alone. As pointed out in Chapter X, both world wars as well as the depression forced a certain amount of industrialization, often haphazard, on all the Latin American countries. Like all the rest of Latin America, Puerto Rico had the bewildering experience of one year being flooded with goods which it could not buy and the next facing shortages so great that it became necessary to make the goods at home.

THE NEW ERA

The changing scene, both political and economic, meant that it became possible, in 1941, not only to make planning an integrated function of the island's new government, but also to count on greatly expanded possibilities for carrying out its findings and recommendations. However, the island's long-established social-economic conditions still imposed serious obstacles.

CAPITAL AND STATE SOCIALISM

While the war removed all danger from the dumping of mainland goods, it did not at the same time create conditions under which capital for industrialization was forthcoming. As elsewhere in the colonial world, those few who had wealth kept it prudently in banks and spent it largely on good living. They were unwilling to invest it in a general program of development which was designed eventually to destroy the social structure within and under which they had become rich. The new government therefore took the stand that if private capital would not build factories, the government would have to do the job. So began the initial stage of industrialization through frank state socialism. When San Juan's leading citizens sent a horrified commission to Washington to demand a military government because Muñoz Marín and Tugwell were leading Puerto Rico straight into "un-American socialism," Muñoz Marín made a remark which can well be used as a guide for all the modern world's emerging societies, laboring to improve their lots but finding it difficult to do so by adhering to doctrinaire methods. "We are neither radical nor conservative," he said, "we are merely realistic."

The cement factory, built by the federal government and turned over to the Puerto Rican, represented the beginning of the industrialization process which is today attracting world attention. In quick succession, as rapidly as machinery and materials could be obtained from the United States, the government now built a factory for making glass bottles, another for making paper and cardboard, a third for the manufacture of such clay products as bricks, tiles, and ceramics, and a fourth for making shoes, while energetically pushing the program of generating electricity and distributing it to all parts of the island, TVA fashion.

POLITICAL ADVANTAGES OF SOCIALISM

The first, "state socialism" phase of industrialization was enormously important in the psychological and so also political sense, if only as tangible proof to Puerto Rico's people that their government meant business. Energetically promoted, it was at the very least a bid for popular support via the "seeing is believing" method which Muñoz Marín was in 1961 to urge on the Alliance for Progress as an important means for capturing the faith of Latin America's masses.

ECONOMIC DISADVANTAGES

On the other hand, government ownership and management of factories proved for a number of reasons to be impractical as a permanent policy. While it was not too difficult for the government to manufacture various products in a socialist fashion, it was far more difficult to distribute them later in a capitalist society. Wages paid in the government factories were dictated by legislative action; they were determined politically rather than economically and were often higher than the industries could bear. By this time the legislature, previously dominated by sugar lawyers, had come to be composed in large measure of labor leaders. For that and other reasons, the government enterprises were peculiarly vulnerable to labor troubles. Even though they paid the highest wages on the island, they were at times tied up by disastrous strikes. While it was obvious that the modernization of agriculture, as well as its decay before modernization, would necessarily reduce employment in that branch of the economy and so create conditions under which ever-increasing numbers would have to be employed in manufacturing and public works, it was equally obvious that the population was growing at a rate which far outstripped the government's ability to acquire capital for financing the industrialization program. Hence, the trend was, in those days, toward ever-increasing unemployment.

THE NEW ECONOMIC POLICY

Early during those years it occurred to a number of Puerto Ricans that while their own available capital, raw materials, and purchasing power were far too limited for a successful industrialization effort, those of the United States proper were not. Rich in resources and purchasing power, the United States economy was generating more than $25 billion worth of new capital every year. If the Puerto Ricans, comprising about 1-½ per cent of the population of the United States, could lure something like one-fifth of one per cent of this new capital into the island's productive effort, and could then manufacture goods for sale largely in the states, though often by converting raw materials imported from the states, the industrialization program could truly be brought to the point where it would every year provide more employment and raise standards of living steadily.

It was obvious, on the other hand, that so drastic a change in basic policy could not be made without preliminary political action. It seemed possible that a program of tax-exemption might be effective in luring American capital to the island, but Governor Tugwell was for some reason opposed to tax exemption and vetoed the legislative bills providing for it. Not until Tugwell had resigned and been replaced by Piñero, and, finally, not until the Puerto Ricans had won the right to elect their own governor who in turn appointed his own cabinet, did the islanders have in their own hands the right and power to shape their own industrialization policies.

THE NEW PROGRAM

Only after the island had strengthened its political base could Puerto Rico begin to take full advantage of its integrated position within the United States economy. Four of the government's factories were sold in 1949 to a Puerto Rican industrialist who has since then made an outstanding success of their operations. The fifth, the shoe factory, was leased to a manufacturer from the mainland United States. Its subsequent success taught an important lesson about markets. The Puerto Rican market had not been able to support the factory because, while the island's people buy many shoes, they buy them in so many styles, shapes, and sizes that one plant cannot possibly turn them all out. Today, making shoes for sale on the mainland, the factory can find a ready market for merely one style of shoe.

ATTRACTIONS FOR CAPITAL

Having sold its own plants, the government set out to attract capital through a number of special concessions. Under present laws, a manufacturer who wishes to establish a new industry in Puerto Rico may be granted ten years' exemption from the Commonwealth's corporate profit taxes, which vary with circumstances but average about 35 per cent as contrasted with the federal profits tax of 52 per cent. Every application is judged on its own merits, but the policy has been established from the start that a manufacturer who wants to close his factory in the states, and so throw workers out of jobs there in order to take advantage of the Puerto Rican offers, is not welcome. Except in special cases, such as petrochemical plants, the manufacturer does not need to invest capital in the construction of a building. The government is erecting such buildings in the few shapes and sizes which it has found to be more or less standard. The manufacturer wanting to establish himself usually finds a building ready for him on his first visit which he can occupy for ten years at reasonable rental. After that period he is expected to buy the building or build a new one. The Government Development Bank lends money at fair interest rates for the purchase of machinery, and if the new manufacturer needs labor with special skills the government will train men in those skills at no cost, on the principle that education is a government function.

THE PROBLEM OF WAGES

While wages are as yet lower in Puerto Rico than on the mainland, and while the high costs of shipping and the like will probably demand that they remain lower, the Puerto Rican government keeps repeating that low wages are not among the baits it holds out to attract investors. Constant efforts are made to raise wages as rapidly as possible. Every two years they are reviewed for groups of industries by a federal board as well as a separate Puerto Rican board; the highest minimum wage recommended by one of those two boards then becomes law. By such means approximately one-third of Puerto Rico's present industries have been brought to the point where they pay the $1.25 per hour minimum decreed by federal law for industries manufacturing goods for interstate commerce. After that point has been reached, the labor unions are expected to achieve further increases through the processes of collective bargaining.

THE PROGRAM'S SUCCESS

The industrialization program began to get under way in its present form about 1950 and has since then resulted in the establishment of more than 800 government-assisted factories on the island, with new plants being inaugurated at an average rate of about 1½ per week. During 1961-62, 275 new factories were opened at an average rate of more than 5 per week. More than 86,000 Puerto Rican workers are now employed in manufacturing under conditions zealously controlled by the government. The fact that almost half of these are women, who now gain more and more economic power after centuries of subjugation, is not only reflected in the island's birth rate, but is a powerful factor in the current social and cultural transformation.

The soundness of the new policies is further attested by the fact that Puerto Rico today experiences one of the highest investment rates found in the capitalist world. Investment in new construction, machinery, and equipment increased from an annual rate of $23 million in 1940 to $367 million in 1959. During the program's early years, the bulk of the investment in manufacturing consisted of mainland capital. However, the growth of bank deposits indicates the rapid formation of local capital. In 1940 these totaled $76 million, and in 1961 $674 million. Approximately half of the capital invested in new manufacturing ventures today comes from Puerto Rico itself.

TYPES OF FACTORIES

While the government welcomes almost any industry, it does put special stress on certain kinds of manufacturing. High on the list of preferences are the metal-working industries and those turning out electric machinery of various kinds; they give much employment and can afford to pay the highest wages. Industries devoted to canning and otherwise processing agricultural products are also given priority in the matter of choice. Favored, too, are those industries whose by-products support others. The business of oil refining, for instance, now supports, with its by-products, a factory making antifreeze fluids for automobiles. A large new flour mill and a rice mill, which receive their imports in bulk from the mainland and then process and pack them, contribute considerably to agricultural development by supplying raw materials for the production of cattle feeds, as does a factory for concentrating and freezing orange and pineapple juices, which dries and grinds the parings of those fruits to produce more cattle-feed.

DISTRIBUTION

Geographically, the new factories show an expected pattern of distribution. Most of them are clustered around San Juan, reaching as far west as Arecibo, eastward toward Fajardo, and south to Caguas, so intensifying the problems there of the Urban Renewal and Housing Corporation, mentioned in Chapter IV. Ponce and its environs form another such cluster.

Government efforts to decentralize industry to the point where every town has its factory have hitherto failed despite incentives in such forms as lower rentals for factory buildings in the more remote towns, as well as promises to extend tax exemption in such towns from 10 years to 13. The reasons for such failures are many and varied. Wives of Continental plant managers are often not content to live in the smaller towns, where opportunities for their social life and for their children's education lag far behind those of San Juan and Ponce. Telephone service, which is still execrable throughout Puerto Rico, in part because it started so and in part because the private telephone company has thus far failed to keep pace with general economic progress, is even worse in the small towns than in the capital. Access to seaports is far more difficult and costly from the inland towns than from cities with their own shipping ports. The inland road system, while outstanding when compared with that of most Latin American Republics, is still, in many regions, increasingly inadequate for handling large, efficient, modern trucks.

PUBLIC WORKS

In general, the situation indicates that Puerto Rico's economic growth has outstripped its progress in public works. In turn, that difficulty led, in 1961, to political action through which Puerto Rico's powers for self-government were widened and strengthened still more.

Public works, the construction of roads and sewers, of schools and waterlines, are financed through public bond issues which must in turn, in order to maintain the government's credit, be held to definite limitations. When the Commonwealth was established in 1952, one of the powers which were *not* passed to the new government was that of limiting the debt-incurring capacity; this was retained by the federal government and was held to a maximum not to exceed 10 per cent of the island's total real estate valuation. Since that limitation was too narrow for the mounting needs, the San Juan legislature petitioned Congress in 1958 to pass to Puerto Rico itself the power to limit its indebtedness. That power was granted in 1961. The Puerto Rican legislature then worked out a plan under which the public indebtedness, beyond that of the autonomous public corporations which float their own bond issues for special purposes, must never surpass a figure which can be serviced for interest and amortization by 15 per cent of the average of the two preceding years' tax receipts, a figure considerably in excess of the former maximum and permitting rapid, immediate acceleration of the public works program. Since the change involved a constitutional amendment, which in turn requires public sanction through a referendum, the voters went to the polls on December 10, 1961, endorsing it overwhelmingly.

(The Puerto Ricans have a romantic predilection for dating the turning points in their emancipation from colonialism to coincide with dates which were significant in the process through which they had become a colony of the United States. "Commonwealth Day," when the present political status went into effect in 1952, is July 25, the day on which, in 1898, General Miles landed in Puerto

Rico with his troops in the course of the Spanish-American War.
December 10, when the Puerto Ricans through a referendum enlarged their freedom still more, is the day on which, in 1898, Spain
formally ceded the island to the United States through the Treaty
of Paris).

UNEMPLOYMENT

In the face of all the remarkable progress in industrialization,
however, the percentage of the labor force remaining unemployed
decreases with aggravating slowness. That condition is due in part
to the growth of the labor force as the total population grows and
in part to the technological unemployment. While Puerto Rico still
suffers from a shortage of skilled labor, constant technological improvements in manufacturing, construction, shipping, and the like
result in decreasing employment at the unskilled end. However,
unemployment, expressed in terms of per cent of the labor force,
must also be equated with the island's emigration, largely to the
United States mainland and primarily to New York. In the past
that migration has played a major role in draining off labor
which was "surplus" to the local productive effect. But the decrease
in emigration mentioned in Chapter IV, from 75,000 in 1952-53 to
below 14,000 in 1960-61, was, on the island, accompanied by a drop
in unemployment, from 16 per cent to 11 per cent of the labor force.
Such figures show unmistakably that Puerto Rico is in fact, slowly
and steadily, winning the battle for employment.

ORGANIZED LABOR

Organized labor plays important, varying, and sometimes hidden
roles in the battle for employment. In the early years of the modern
transformation, labor regarded government mills, government
farms, government factories primarily as devices for taking up the
unemployment slack by creating a maximum number of jobs. Every
move to improve efficiency through technological changes, or by
the direct means of cutting down unduly large labor forces, was
likely to be countered by a costly strike and called for accelerated
governmental efforts in the important field of labor education. By
today, organized labor has by and large come to realize that tech-

nological unemployment is inevitable because economic enterprises, governmental or private, cannot succeed in competition with all the rest of the world except by constantly improving their productive efficiency.

GOVERNMENT LABOR POLICIES

In Puerto Rico there is no basic conflict between the government and organized labor similar to that found in dictatorships. The government encourages unions and urges them to do everything legally possible to increase wages beyond the minima set by government action. The Department of Labor's record of successful conciliation and arbitration in disputes between labor and management compares favorably with that of all the federated states. On the other hand, Puerto Rico's organized unions are still relatively weak, primarily because elsewhere dramatic gains in labor's status had largely to be achieved through militant union action while in Puerto Rico they were achieved by the government, through legislative action, without waiting for strikes. However, Puerto Rico's unions are now becoming more sophisticated and are gaining in strength. Also, they remain honest. While Hoffa and others of his kind have in recent years made some progress in capturing sections of the local labor movement, they find the going difficult because they are working in a society which began to learn in 1940 not to sell its votes and to be increasingly suspicious of demagogy. Despite all their bombast about the obvious wage differentials between Puerto Rico and the federated states, despite the considerable sums they have spent in their efforts to gain a strong foothold on the island, the racketeers have so far made little progress. On the other hand, mainland unions such as the International Ladies' Garment Workers, recognizing Puerto Rico's peculiar situations under which equality with the mainland in matters of wages is impossible, have gained considerably in influence.

POLITICAL IMPLICATIONS

With all its remarkable economic growth, Puerto Rico is today still twice as poor, or only half as rich, as is Mississippi, the Union's poorest state. Its per capita average annual income, which has been multiplied by more than five in two decades, remains only half of Mississippi's, as does its budget in per capita terms. The question of how a change in political status would affect economic growth is therefore always uppermost in the local political debate.

As shown in Chapter VI, Puerto Rico's present development is based solidly on a "tripod" composed of the three legs: free trade with the United States, exemption from contributions to the federal treasury, and political freedom to use such arrangements for the optimum benefit of all concerned. Independence, as shown in Chapter VI, would deprive the island of its free United States markets. Obviously, federated statehood would deprive it of exemption from federal taxation while greatly curtailing its present powers to manage its own affairs. As a commonwealth Puerto Rico has far more freedom in fiscal affairs than it would have as a state.

In the political debate on relations with the United States, the leaders of the Statehood Republican Party, while obviously eager to win an election regardless of status, seem also to regard Puerto Rico's potential federated statehood as a certain protection against the independence which, while legally still possible, would be economically suicidal. They do, however, also advance economic arguments which seem to show that statehood would cost the island relatively little in money or would even, depending on the moment's mood or the statistics quoted, benefit it economically. The reply of those, comprising the party in power, who advocate the retention and strengthening of the present status as a permanent arrangement runs approximately as follows:

If Puerto Rico were a state, its citizens would have to pay federal income taxes in addition to local, which are approximately on a par with the federal. While their individual tax burdens would be doubled, a considerable number of the industries which provide the money would undoubtedly have to depart from the island. Whether able or not, they would have to abide by the federal minimum wage laws; tax-exemption would be a thing of the past since the federal government would take 52 per cent of the annual profits. Puerto Rican customs receipts and federal excise taxes on such things as rum and cigars made on the island would go to the federal treasury instead of, as now, to Puerto Rico's.

In 1960, the United States Bureau of the Budget studied the situation and reported that if Puerto Rico had been a state the previous year such statehood would have cost $188 million in addition to the cost of running local affairs. While the island's budget in 1959 was about $230 million, its receipts from internal taxes were about $180 million, the remainder coming from other sources. In other words, Puerto Rico's tax burden, already high and difficult to collect, would have to be more than doubled under statehood while an appreciable part of the economy would, for that reason and others, necessarily collapse.

"And what would we get out of it?" asked some of the island's leaders. "Two Senators and six Representatives in the United States Congress. Since when are eight politicians worth $188 million per year?"

Culture, Education and Health

CULTURE

THE leaders who framed Puerto Rico's present political status as a "Free, Associated State" were well aware of the need for maintaining the cultural cohesion and identity from which a society, in the last analysis, derives its strength. They knew that, as an independent republic, Puerto Rico would seem to have the best chance of maintaining its own culture. However, its chances for economic growth, or even survival, would be so slim that the culture could hardly remain viable. As a state, they feared, Puerto Rico would have to give up its cultural identity. English would undoubtedly have to become the official language, and the island's people would have to choose between being "Americanized" in a hurry, in many subtle ways strange to them, or suffer the fate of so many Mexicans in the United States Southwest, as second-class citizens, alien and often despised. They argued that only under commonwealth status as a self-governing people voluntarily collaborating with the United States in solving the knotty problem of centuries-old colonialism, could Puerto Rico's people retain their cultural pride and use it as a solid foundation from which to "borrow" the many new culture-traits demanded by their social and economic transformation.

Today, the dwindling number of Puerto Ricans who continue to demand independence are precisely those who most stubbornly insist on keeping old culture values alive in all their purity, while resenting the influx of new "American" ways. "What has happened," they ask nostalgically, "to the fine old ways of life, when the family was supreme, when our demands were simpler, when we sat in coffee houses, wrote poems and sang songs, happy and proud as Puerto Ricans?" "Those old ways," reply their political opponents, "went the way of universal hunger, of street gangs of homeless waifs, of illness, bad housing, and lack of opportunity." At the other end of the political spectrum, those who clamor for federated statehood within the American Union are most often the men and women at the social top or in the fast-growing middle class, some of whom strive to reject their own culture as Puerto Ricans and wish, as rapidly as possible and often for reason of personal gain or security, to become "Americans" in a society of Americans, made over into a semblance of "the American way of life."

While that culture-war, as reflected in politics, is a strong but not always visible undercurrent in Puerto Rico's modern life, the government does all it can to encourage and help those Puerto Ricans who have migrated to New York and other mainland centers to learn English, join labor unions, participate in politics (if only as voters), and integrate themselves as rapidly as they can into the once-alien life and culture in which they have chosen to take root.

Puerto Rico's culture struggle is symptomatic of that which underlies all true revolutions, including modern Latin America's which the Alliance for Progress is designed to abet. For that reason and others, Puerto Rico is invaluable to Kennedy's hemispheral policies as an example of a Latin American society which the United States once, under colonialism, tried unsuccessfully to "Americanize," but is today helping to maintain and strengthen its own culture.

CULTURAL VIABILITY

A society's culture, the many-faceted expression of its people's cohesion and sense of identity, must be constantly in a state of flux to remain viable. One of colonialism's most tragic effects is the psychological and cultural erosion of its victims as their creative drives and urges are impeded through restraints imposed by the rulers. To some extent, all colonial subjects have been driven underground in the cultural sense, and their creative drives and urges wait only to burst forth.

During the nearly four centuries of Spanish rule, the wide gulf between the Spanish overlords in San Juan and their Puerto Rican subjects slowly compelled the growth of a truly Puerto Rican culture which, poor as it might be, Spanish as were its language and historic origins, differentiated the Puerto Ricans from their Iberian masters. Not until the nineteenth century were the Puerto Ricans permitted to have their own newspapers and their own cultural societies in which they were free to discuss mathematics, philosophy, and the arts, but not politics. The nineteenth century was also the first which saw the emergence of true "Puerto Rican" poets, artists, philosophers. For a brief moment, in 1898, the establishment of the autonomous government promised them a measure of even greater freedom to develop and grow along lines of their own choosing. Then the Spanish-American War swept them back again to their former status as colonial subjects, this time under a culture alien to them.

CULTURE CONFLICTS

The ancient rift between the Puerto Ricans and their Spanish rulers was now widened and transformed into one between them and their Anglo-American overlords. To be sure, a number of Puerto Ricans, most of them businessmen who were ashamed of their own indigenous culture, welcomed their new masters and did everything in their power, willy-nilly and usually with ridiculous results, to take on "American" ways, talk with unbridled fervor about Washington, Jefferson, and Lincoln, and become "Americans" at least superficially. Many others, however, bitterly resented the facts that they had no voice in shaping the governmental policies which regulated their lives, that they could not aspire to top positions in North American and European firms operating on the island, that the North Americans as a class held themselves aloof from the Puerto Ricans, and that the Washington government attempted to use the school system for the purpose of "Americanizing" the children.

Meanwhile, however, the great masses of Puerto Ricans, and especially the rural poor, accepted their lots stoically. Long accustomed to their lives as beggars at the door of their imperial rulers, they clung to their own patterns of living, sang their own songs and composed new ones as occasions arose, danced their own dances, celebrated their saint's birthdays at fiesta time, and ignored the "Americanos" to as great an extent as possible.

When Muñoz Marín won the election of 1940 with the promise that now the Puerto Ricans, their leaders and people, would begin to take hold of their own affairs, to shape their destinies as Puerto Ricans, he also set off a great explosion of energy with its inevitable reflections in a revitalized culture. As it became evident during the decades which followed that the Puerto Ricans would have to amend their culture through many "borrowings" from the United States and elsewhere, it became equally evident to the intellectuals and leaders that only by retaining and strengthening their sense of identity, only by retaining and strengthening their native culture and their pride in it, could they effectively carry on the task of transforming their lives and their society and could they indulge in cultural borrowings without the risk of being engulfed and losing their identity. Not all Puerto Ricans, of course, feel like that. The new middle class which has grown by leaps and bounds during the past decade or two contains thousands of members who seem to want nothing but to conform, to buy new automobiles and go into debt for new freezers, washing machines, and other gadgets.

OPERATION SERENITY

To counteract such trends, Muñoz Marín talks about "Operation Serenity," exhorting his people not to be carried away by the shabby instinct for mere acquisition for its own sake. Indeed, he has devised three "operations" for modern Puerto Rico, corresponding to the three sacred rights listed in the Declaration of Independence. "Operation Bootstrap," concerned with the improvement of living standards through economic development, corresponds to the Declaration's "Life"; "Operation Commonwealth," devoted to political emancipation, corresponds to "Liberty"; "Operation Serenity" is equated with the "Pursuit of Happiness."

The present government is deeply concerned with strengthening and guiding Puerto Rico's culture. The Institute of Puerto Rican Culture was established as a government agency in 1955. Its many programs deal with such matters as archeology, music, literature, the stage, architecture, painting, and the like. The Department of Parks and Recreation, beside providing such things as baseball fields presents Spanish-language plays in various parts of the island, admission gratis, and gives courses in dramatics, folk dancing, and native music. The Department of Education manages a radio and television station devoted entirely to cultural matters, with no advertising and no politics. The station broadcasts a number of courses through which college credits may be earned, many newscasts and discussions, and the concerts of the annual Casals Music Festival. Pablo Casals, since moving to Puerto Rico from France in 1956, has done a great deal to stimulate the island's interest in the world's great music. In addition to establishing the annual festivals, he has organized a Puerto Rico Symphony Orchestra and founded a conservatory of music. Every season the symphony orchestra plays a number of concerts out-of-doors, with attendance free, to give the poor an opportunity to hear the best music.

The Department of Education's Division of Community Education works with outstanding success in the rural areas, using its own techniques to arouse people to take an interest in their immediate problems and to solve those problems through self-developed community programs for building bridges, providing safe water supplies, building roads, planting community gardens, and the like. The cultural renaissance is also being carried to the people in trucks. "Bookmobiles," or traveling public libraries, make the rounds day after day, month in and month out. There is at least one mobile museum, its large truck loaded with Puerto Rican cultural exhibits, while the university's "Rolling Theater" brings plays to the rural areas.

EDUCATION

In the final analysis, a people's culture, its ways of living, its aspirations, are reflected in its educational system. However, being controlled by those who hold the political power, that system reflects *their* ideas of what the culture is or should be while also being used to intrench, if not their rule, then the system of government represented by it. In times of rapid culture change, as in both Puerto Rico and the United States today, when nobody has the prescience to foresee tomorrow's realities, educators are likely to quarrel over such things as philosophies, curricula, and methodologies.

EDUCATION AND POLITICS

The history of Puerto Rico's education is that of its political vicissitudes. Before 1820 it was entirely in the hands of the clergy, church-controlled, church-oriented, taking the well-to-do through the equivalent of secondary schools in theological matters, doling out instructions to a few of the poor in smaller doses and as a matter of charity. Then, at last, Spain began to take an interest in education in the two islands which were left to it in the crumbling Spanish-American empire. Increasingly the Spanish government came to regard Puerto Rico's educational system as a political arm through which to spread its doctrines and intrench its rule. However, the autonomous constitution which went into effect on February 11, 1898, could at last declare that a colonial government had the full right to establish its own system of education. That freedom, granted by Spain, was swept aside within a few months when the United States took hold of the educational system, and was not regained until after 1948.

When the United States stepped into the picture, the educational system was still crude, orthodox, and church-dominated. Only a small percentage of the children of school age actually received instruction. Approximately 85 per cent of the population was illiterate. With admirable energy, the Washington government undertook to combat the social scourge of illiteracy while also, however, setting out to use the school system primarily for the purpose of "Americanizing" the islanders as rapidly as possible. Dr. G. M. Brumbaugh, the first Commissioner of Education under the American flag, a man fanatically devoted to salutes to the flag and lusty renderings by the children of such patriotic songs as *America, Hail Columbia,* and *The Star-Spangled Banner,* reported after only one year's efforts that the average Puerto Rican child already knew more about Washington, Lincoln, Betsy Ross, and the American flag than did the average child in the United States. It was decreed very early during United States rule that all the teaching in all the schools must be done in English, a matter which led to much confusion because the teachers themselves knew little or no English, and the children were expected to learn the three R's in a language utterly alien to them. Only those children who had both a flair for learning a language and teachers adept in that language survived the first few grades; the rest, regarded as stupid, dropped out and intensified their typical colonial feelings of inferiority opposite their imperial rulers.

The teachers resented the system, not only as bad pedagogy, but also as an insult to Puerto Rico's culture and *dignidad*. Before alien heads of the school system, however, who had the power of dismissal, they kept prudently quiet. Only slowly did it become apparent to the Washington government that its early policies were not working well. In 1930, Hoover appointed Dr. José Padín as Commissioner of Education. An able and progressive educator, Padín began immediately to re-examine the island's educational philosophy, to study Puerto Rico's needs, and to encourage his teachers to do the same. That was the turning point for a trend which has not yet run its full course: a turning away from tradition in theory, and routine in practice, toward a system based on studied realities and resulting needs. Under Padín a system was inaugurated in which the teaching in elementary and secondary schools was done in Spanish, though English was a required subject of study. It worked well until, in 1936, the Nationalists began their campaign of assassination and frightened the Washington authorities.

Senator King of Utah, then head of the Senate's Committee on Insular Affairs, visited Puerto Rico to conduct an investigation of his own. He correlated the prevailing unrest and anti-American feeling with the fact that he found few children who could speak English, and began, immediately on his return to Washington, to use his Senatorial powers to enforce a "get-tough-about-English" policy. Padín's resignation was accepted. His successor, who had had to commit himself in writing on the matter of stressing English as a prerequisite for senatorial endorsement, had an extremely difficult time and resigned in 1945.

TROUBLED EMERGENCE

The Popular Democratic Party, which had been in power since 1941, now set out to find somebody to formulate and lead a new educational policy adequate for its revolution's needs. The United States Senate, however, remained adamant in its demand that any candidate commit himself in writing to the stressing of English. The need for adequate English instruction was obvious to all concerned. However, no qualified candidate would sign such a pledge, which took the matter of such instruction out of skilled pedagogic hands and made it a political matter. The island's educational system was without a responsible head until after 1948, when the first governor ever to be elected by the people also acquired the power to appoint his own cabinet without consulting the United States Senate.

The former "Commissioner" now became the "Secretary of Education." The first was Dr. Mariano Villaronga, who immediately tackled the enormous task of shaping the educational system to fit the island's mounting needs. The task is far from completed, in part because the needs keep changing, in part because there is still disagreement as to their nature. While the present commonwealth status permits the Puerto Rican people to retain their cultural identity and Spanish language, it also demands that they become bilingual as rapidly as possible and even, in a sense, bi-cultural. Though widely acknowledged, that need also leads to much dissention as to ways and means. The public schools have returned to an adaptation of the former Padín system of teaching in Spanish but making English a required subject of study; teachers are sent to the states on scholarships to perfect their knowledge of English. So far, however, the gains have been slow and the results insufficient.

According to jingoistic journalists from the states, as well as members of Muñoz Marín's political opposition, this "proves" that the present government is secretly plotting to lead Puerto Rico into independence. Those who advocate heavier stress on English because Puerto Ricans migrating to the states have a difficult time without it are attacked with the charge that they want to use the school system for training Puerto Ricans "for export" rather than for taking hold of their affair at home. Meanwhile the Catholic parochial schools, being able to import highly trained nuns from the states, can do a much better job than can the public school system in teaching English.

Advisory missions and experts have studied the educational system, or parts of it, from time to time, with varying results. Meanwhile the debate still flares up between those who insist on strengthening Puerto Rico's culture, those who maintain that education must return to its former task of "Americanization," and those who have their loving eyes on Western culture as expressed through the hundred best books while at least seeming to claim that Puerto Rico, never having produced a Shakespeare or participated in a Battle of Waterloo, has neither culture nor history.

VOCATIONAL TRAINING

The phenomenal growth of manufacturing in what was only yesterday a backward agricultural society creates pressing problems of vocational training. After World War II, the government bought a mass of surplus war equipment and used it to found, in San Juan, what was then the world's largest vocational school; it has since been decentralized, with branches in various parts of the island. Thousands of students now take courses in a wide variety of trades, ranging from aviation mechanics through cabinet-making to beauty parlor operations. Similarly, a "Hotel School" turns out trained employees to serve the growing tourist industry.

THE NEED FOR FUNDS

One-third of the Commonwealth's total budget today goes for education, but the need for ever more money keeps mounting. The salaries of teachers are admittedly too low. Despite an accelerated construction program, there are still not enough classrooms to meet current needs. More than 80 per cent of the teachers in the elementary grades have to cope with the "double enrollment" system under which they handle one class for some three hours every morning and another for the same amount of time in the afternoon. Hitherto there has simply not been enough money available for meeting the rising needs. Now the transfer, from the federal government to the Puerto Rican, of the power to limit the island's public debt, discussed in Chapter VIII and resulting in considerable enlargement of the debt-incurring capacity, will permit a corresponding acceleration of the program for building schools and the like.

CONCRETE RESULTS

While many problems remain to be solved, the energy with which the Puerto Ricans are tackling their education is attested by the fact that the total enrollment in schools of all kinds, from elementary institutions to the university, rose from 302,428 in 1940 to almost 750,000 in 1960. The University of Puerto Rico itself grew from a student body of 4,987 in 1940 to one of 18,223 in 1960. According to a United Nations report of 1957, 29.9 per cent of Puerto Rico's total population was then enrolled in the elementary, secondary, and vocational schools. The figure was the world's highest; that for the United States, 22.2 per cent, came next. Illiteracy among those ten years of age or older was 31.5 per cent in 1940, 12.4 per cent in 1960. It is dropping rapidly today as older people die or go to special night classes, and promises within another decade or so to disappear entirely.

PUBLIC HEALTH

The facts that, throughout the public school system, special stress is placed on instruction in health and hygiene, and that (with federal assistance) substantial free lunches are served daily to all the pupils throughout the school year, have much to do with the phenomenal improvements in public health which have been observed in Puerto Rico in recent decades.

The island serves as one of many modern refutations of the old concept that the humid tropics, because their climates are favorable for the propagation of insects and other disease vectors, must necessarily have disease rates higher than those in the so-called temperate regions. The claim has long been answered by those who pointed out that the tropics have too long been colonial regions par excellence, that they have therefore lacked the individual and public financial means which are available in more favored lands for combating diseases, and that their poor showing in matters of public health was therefore due to the man-made climate of exploitative colonialism rather than to the natural climate. Officials in the U.S. Public Health Service have long expressed that concept succinctly when they said that: "Public health is a purchasable commodity; you get what you pay for." Dr. Juan Pons, for years Puerto Rico's outstanding and imaginative Secretary of Health, said: "There is no such thing as tropical medicine. There is merely a medicine of low standards of living and another of higher."

DISEASE PATTERNS AND SOCIAL CHANGES

In line with that dictum, it is notable that Puerto Rico's entire disease pattern has changed since an energetic government set out to better the people's lives by improving standards of living steadily together with the diets which strengthen resistance to disease, making increasing amounts of money available for public health purposes, and creating conditions under which imagination and invention were encouraged. Before 1940, Puerto Rico's three greatest killers were, in the order given: diarrhea and enteritis, tuberculosis, and malaria. By today, malaria has been eliminated entirely, and the rates for the other two have gone down so notably that they can no longer be regarded as scourges. Today the two most serious causes of death are diseases of rising standards of living with their concomitant aging populations: heart disease and cancer. Meanwhile, as pointed out in Chapter IV, the island's crude (not corrected for age distribution) death rate dropped from 18.2 per thousand in 1940 to 6.6. in 1960, while the life expectancy rose from 46 to 68 years and the per capita average annual income from $121 to $565. Taken together, such figures, as mirrors of Puerto Rico's experiences, bear out the dictum in Howard Craig's book *Introduction to Social Medicine* that "Medicine is an integral, interrelated, and interdependent part of a functioning social and economic system which, to be viable, must exist in a continuing state of flux."

HEALTH PROBLEMS

Outstanding among the problems confronting the health officials in and since 1940 are: (1) the shortage of physicians, and (2) the people's relative poverty and consequent inability to pay for medical services. Between 1940 and 1959, the number of physicians available on the island rose from 509, with 3,672 persons per physician, to 1,953, serving an average of 1,181 persons each. The recent establishment of a School of Medicine within the university promises a rapid increase in the medical services available, though the problem of keeping the graduates on the island in the face of greener financial pastures in the mainland states is still serious. The public's relatively low purchasing power means that about 80 per cent of the medicine must still be public medicine, dispensed through public hospitals and the excellent free clinics and health centers which have been established in all the towns. However, now that purchasing power is rising, that situation in turn gives rise to debate in medical circles over "socialized medicine" and to much public speculation on the problem of how to prevent abuses through being more strict than formerly about extracting payment from those who are able to pay.

ILLNESS AND PATTERNS OF LIVING

The lamentable health conditions prevailing some decades ago bore out the claim that illness is an integrated part of a way of life, whereas diseases reflect unsatisfactory manners of living. The fact that the rural poor, in general, lacked outhouses meant that vast areas of ground and most streams were polluted. Too poor to buy shoes or to live on diesease-resisting diets, the people were prey to the hookworm whose parasite is transmitted through the soles of the feet. Earlier drives to combat the disease through dosing the patients with medicine proved futile; no sooner were people purged of the parasites than they picked them up again. During the worst of the depression years, 1933, there were 770 deaths from ancylostomiasis (hookworm), or 46.8 per 100,000 people. Since 1956, no deaths whatever from the disease have been recorded. The change was due only in part to accelerated medical services and improved diets. It was due more specifically to the government's drive to improve the general sanitary environment, including a massive and successful program for the construction of outhouses, as well as the distribution of shoes through the educational system.

WATER SUPPLIES

Urban water supplies have by now been entirely cleaned up. In San Juan itself, where a few decades ago it was highly advisable to boil and filter all water used for domestic purposes, the city water supply has since 1950 been certified for interstate commerce, which means that any steamer or airplane may fill up its tanks with it without taking special precautions.

In the rural areas, the women of a few decades ago had often to go long distances to fetch their domestic water from rivers and springs which were generally polluted, thereby exposing themselves and their families to a number of ailments, including the dread and incurable bilharzia which is propagated through fresh water snails. Today the program for a good sanitary environment includes the construction of hundreds of miles of "rural aqueducts" or pipes through which safe, potable water is brought free to conveniently located taps, available to hundreds of thousands of rural inhabitants, while the research-and-combative drive on bilharzia, going hand in hand with an educational campaign, is showing marked results.

It is by such methods, speeded up year by year as means and manpower become increasingly available, that Puerto Rico has by now reduced its death rate to a point lower than that of the United States as a whole. When contemplating that rate of 6.6 per thousand per year, it is interesting to note that the Soviet Union has recently begun to brag that its own death rate of 7.5 per thousand is "the world's lowest."

T<small>HE</small> Commonwealth Department of State, in collaboration with that of the United States and at times with the United Nations, private concerns, or directly with foreign governments, carries out several programs under which foreign visitors and trainees come to Puerto Rico in a steady stream to observe the Puerto Rican effort or a number of its specific aspects. These programs, to which Puerto Rico itself contributes a considerable amount of money out of its own limited funds, were inaugurated in 1950, shortly after President Truman had made his epoch-making "Point IV" declaration. Proposed by the Puerto Ricans themselves, the programs are regarded as a means through which Puerto Rico can express its indebtedness to the United States by contributing to that country's good reputation and combating the stubbornly reiterated charge that it is an imperialistic nation, greedily bent on the subjugation and exploitation of all lesser peoples within its avid reach.

By June 30, 1961, Puerto Rico had received 15,218 official visitors under those programs. Coming largely from Latin America, the Caribbean area, Asia, Africa, and Oceania, the visitors had included some Europeans plus a considerable sprinkling of United States officials and technicians preparing to go abroad to further the "Point IV" movement of technical and financial assistance to the non-communist world's "emerging" societies. The visitors represented no fewer than 126 separate countries, including all the Latin American nations. Truly, Puerto Rico has become a showcase for democratic progress and a laboratory for the ubiquitous current revolutionary social changes aimed at improving standards of living and strengthening democracy.

The official visitors, who continue to arrive in Puerto Rico in a steady stream, come for various reasons and carry home with them a variety of impressions.

An appreciable number of them are journalists who have heard conflicting descriptions of Puerto Rico, on the one hand as a "land of wonders" and on the other as a stricken suffering colony of Yanqui imperialism. They are encouraged to visit the island to form their own impressions.

Others, especially from Latin America and the Caribbean area, stay in Puerto Rico for protracted periods, on scholarships, to study at the university or to learn a variety of trades ranging from printing to electronics.

At a higher level, but for briefer visits and primarily for the purpose of gaining general impressions, come distinguished technicians and officials of dozens of countries throughout the non-communist world. Some of these, more interested in methodologies than philosophies, observe the ways in which Puerto Rico handles various problems. Some find ideas of value to their own countries. Some, especially those who come from countries like Israel, contribute ideas of value to Puerto Rico. A few, observing that the Puerto Rican program was tailored specifically to fit the island's realities and needs, dismiss it impatiently as having nothing to offer the countries which do not enjoy Puerto Rico's unique relationship with its former imperial rulers. Every now and then a visitor with leftist orientations announces that what is happening on the island is merely a new, disguised, and diabolically subtle form of imperial subjugation and exploitation.

However, many foreign visitors recognize in the Puerto Rican experience a variation of their own as peoples emerging from the anguish of their former colonialism. To such observers what is happening in the Commonwealth today is not so much a series of more or less isolated programs and projects as an explosion of the human spirit, an inspiring human experience through which vast new energies are released to seek new paths, new definitions of old concepts, new human values to serve a new age of ubiquitous social transformations.

Finally there are observers who see in Puerto Rico a symbol of new trends through which the stream of human history, veering sharply in the modern age, is taking brand new directions and is sweeping along all human societies, their own included. To such observers Puerto Rico, with its colonial background, is of tremendous value to the rest of the fast-changing world. They realize clearly that when President Kennedy spoke of the present Latin American "revolution" he was in effect speaking of the entire noncommunist world and especially of the world of former colonies.

THE DEPRESSION AND COLONIALISM

The world depression signalled the end of colonialism as an institution of capitalism, not only in Puerto Rico but elsewhere as well. The many new nations today rising from the ashes of yesterday's colonial empires would have emerged as surely, and perhaps even more rapidly, had there never been a World War II, followed by the so-called "Cold War," and had the Germans not sent Lenin into Russia in a sealed train in 1917.

PRODUCTION VERSUS CONSUMPTION

While oversimplification is dangerous, especially in an historic era of universal seething change and immense complexity, it is sometimes useful. The world depression, when the term "underconsumption" battled against "over-production" in the war of slogans, when the United States was plagued by some millions of unemployed workers and their families, with Europe's industrial nations in the same desperate predicament, was a time when capitalism had to take serious stock of its own shortcomings lest it give way to a system of rigid political and economic rule. In the writings and speeches of those years, the talks at chambers of commerce, at banquets attended by leading manufacturers, everywhere slowly and timidly and often painfully emerged one basic idea: capitalism had reached the point where its production of a multiplicity of goods had far outstripped the production of customers with the wherewithal for buying those goods. While factories and warehouses were choked with automobiles and refrigerators, with idle stockpiles of metals, with bottled drinks and cosmetics which could not be sold, creditors and stockholders were nevertheless forced to demand interest, amortization, and dividends. The institution of capitalism with its attendant political democracy was therefore threatened with collapse.

Stated bluntly and without overtones of generosity, idealism, and the Christian spirit, the problem was to create millions of new customers with reasonable purchasing power. It was not the first time the problem had arisen in those terms. Who can say that the abolition of slavery was not prompted in part by the dawning realization that slaves, while constituting cheap labor, are also poor customers? Who can say that the present accelerated trend toward "emancipation" of the American Negroes is not part and parcel of the same movement to create more power to purchase the products of factories? Early during the world depression it became obvious that Puerto Rico's cane cutters, those who were employed at miserable, starvation wages and those who had lost their jobs, constituted a drain on the public's relief funds while contributing pitifully little to the economy. Those cane cutters, and African colonial subjects working for 17 cents per day, and Asia's poverty-stricken plantation workers, not to mention Latin America's feudal serfs, who were multiplying at an alarming rate which outstripped by far feudalism's ability to provide them with the barest essentials, could not even buy shoes and shirts, to say nothing of books, bicycles, cars, refrigerators, Coca-Cola, stocks and bonds, tooth brushes, education, and public health.

THE INTELLECTUAL REVOLUTION

The task of reshaping capitalism's world for the purpose of saving capitalism itself entails an enormous intellectual revolution, which is only now getting under way. Many old ideas and concepts, old basic premises in geography, sociology, and all the other social sciences, which had formerly served to uphold the imperialistic colonialism from which so many had sprung, had to be re-examined and transformed into new guiding concepts designed to serve modern needs more adequately. Just as the modern emergence of new weapons of war has forced geographers to redefine their former ideas of strategic location, so the emergence of Africans into positions of dignity and power has forced the critical re-examination of many former, deeply intrenched notions about racial superiority and inferiority, to say nothing of such socially dangerous bodies of thought as those dealing with "over-population" and the "debilitating" climate of the world's tropical regions. The deeply rooted idea that the benefits of industrialized production belongs primarily and even exclusively to the white Caucasians who invented it, had to be, and is being, subjected to a minute, skeptical scrutiny.

Today's mounting intellectual renaissance, as yet held in check by the special and specious kinds of thinking inspired by the Cold War, is vitalized by the terrible, dawning realization that man's science, as Muñoz Marín once put it, has at last outstripped his wisdom for guiding its use. Spurred by desperate necessity, the modern renaissance promises to surpass that of another age, which, also arising from agony and travail, produced new and workable concepts of geography, the cosmology of Copernicus, the book of logarithms, and Shakespeare's plays.

POPULATION PRESSURES

The world depression showed clearly that the entire capitalist world with its empires was "over-populated" as indicated by such criteria as hunger, misery, illness, ignorance, and accompanying discontent. Quite aside from communism's lure under such conditions, and quite aside from communism's endlessly reiterated charges that a heartless capitalism wants only to squeeze the last drops of blood out of its colonial subjects, it became obvious that the economy had to expand quickly to provide for those who seemed, under prevailing conditions to be surplus to the land.

President Roosevelt, one of the modern day's greatest crusaders against colonialism, attempted to handle his desperate Puerto Rican problem, first with federal relief and later with an enlightened kind of "reconstruction" under which the island's economy was to be changed through federal action in such a manner as to serve the island's people better than it had served them formerly. But if Roosevelt ran into trouble he was also the first to recognize, in Puerto Rico, the truth of what Chester Bowles was to write in 1955: "For all that it accomplished as the local adjunct of the New Deal in the nineteen thirties, the Puerto Rico Reconstruction Administration early demonstrated the ineffectiveness of a rigid planning which was benevolently prepared and supervised by a government

outside the immediate context of local needs. Thus a decade ago
Puerto Ricans learned a lesson which should now be a truism: that
if a people are to be saved from whatever danger threatens them,
whether it be the militant aggression of communism or the social
scourge of poverty and disease, they will in the last analysis save
themselves through their own indigenous power, pride, and respon-
sibility. If outsiders are to be helpful, their help must take the form
of friendly and unobtrusive support." [1]

In a special sense, and again within the special reasoning of oversimplification, overpopulation also triggered Europe's last great
intellectual renaissance, the inspiring stirrings of a host of eminent
men from Prince Henry the Navigator through Columbus, Copernicus, Galileo, Walter Raleigh, Humphrey Gilbert, Shakespeare,
and others, all of them reaching for new values and finding them in
widely-varying degrees. Feudalism, like colonialism today, had apparently reached the end of its rope. A feudal estate can support
only so many serfs; when these multiply beyond the estate's capacity
to keep them alive and working, their offspring become a dangerous *Lumpenproletariat,* crowding fields, highways, and city slums.
Europe's terrible sufferings after the eleventh century, its famines,
dreadful epidemics, and wars (including the Thirty Years' War,
which devastated vast areas in the holy cause of proving that two
socio-economic-religious systems which still, perforce, flourish side
by side, could not live together in the same world), were symptoms
of over-population. Successive crusades failed to find new *Lebens-
raum* in the east. Eventually, inevitably, the age of exploration
opened vast new realms in the Americas and elsewhere, in which
medieval feudalism could survive yet another few centuries.

LATIN AMERICA AND ANGLO-AMERICA

So began the rift between Latin America and Anglo-America
which must today finally be closed and for the closing of which
Kennedy announced his Alliance for Progress. The Iberian nations,
with their geographic monopolies granted by the Pope, could han-

[1] From Chester Bowles' introduction to *Transformation, the Story of Modern
Puerto Rico,* by Earl Parker Hanson.

dle their population problems without drastically changing their feudal economies. Among Europe's many imports into the New World immediately after Columbus' voyages, the related institutions of feudalism and Catholicism were the most important. The conquerors, who, like Pizarro, may have been swineherds in Europe, became the aristocratic, ruling overlords while the native Indians became the feudal serfs, augmented here and there in the lowland tropics by Negro slaves.

THE RISE OF CAPITALISM

Northwestern Europe, prevented for a time by Papal decrees and other realities from joining the massive exodus into the New World, had perforce to reshape its economies to accommodate its teeming and growing populations. Feudalism began slowly to give way to capitalism and industrialism, bolstered and strengthened by new Protestant religious systems. The once-heretical idea of human dignity, going hand in hand with individual freedom, began to take root, burgeoning slowly in soils that were often barren and rocky. Today differences between Latin America and Anglo-America stem in part from differences in timing. The Pilgrims landed at Plymouth Rock more than a century after the Spaniards had established themselves in Hispaniola and Puerto Rico. During that century they had developed a brand new set of ideas which were anathema to the feudal Spaniards and had much to do with the savage seventeenth-century fighting between the two worlds in which Puerto Rico played so important a role.

The difference between the Anglo-American and Latin American revolutions indicates wide cultural differences. The North American revolution was fought in large measure for the right of every man to life, liberty, and the pursuit of happiness. While lip-service was given to those rights in Latin America, Simón Bolivars' revolutionary wars were in effect fought for the freedom of the upper classes to continue and strengthen their feudalism without interference from Spain in such matters as political powers and trade. While the United States developed into the world's greatest industrial nation, its democracy marred for a time by slavery in the

South with its tragic human aftermaths, Latin America, with few exceptions (such as Costa Rica), remained for a century the great stronghold of feudalism in the Western hemisphere. Its ruling upper classes resisted at every step such social advances as economic diversification, education, health services, and geographic expansion into the remaining frontier areas.

FEUDAL ECONOMIES

Throughout the better part of a century, the Latin American nations fell into the Adam Smith category of those which must produce raw materials, including foods, for sale to the industrial nations, whose finished products were in turn to be bought by the less developed societies. When more and more capital was required for the extraction of raw materials, while population growth in Latin America called for the creation of ever-increasing numbers of new jobs, the feudal aristocrats saved themselves as such for yet another while by giving exploitative concessions to foreign capital, particularly North American. Latin America's transportation pattern, its railroads laid out almost exclusively from inland areas to the sea to facilitate the export of raw materials but not internal development, remained typically "colonial" in nature. The foreign concessionaries who produced copper, oil, processed meats, etc., could hardly help but be "exploiters," regardless of whether or not they liked it. Had they acted otherwise, had they been markedly less exploitative than were the feudal lords who ran the local governments, they would have been expelled from their respective positions.

Throughout that period of Latin America's history, the populations grew far more rapidly than did the economies sustaining them.

WORLD UPHEAVALS

During World War I, the producers of raw materials had the wherewithal for purchasing industrialism's finished products but could not get them because of war shortages in goods and ships. This was a crisis period which saw accelerated efforts at local industrialization. In this respect it resembled the world depression, which curtailed purchasing power, and World War II, which again curtailed the availability of industrial products. Inevitably, Latin America was forced by world movements into its own industrial revolution, always too little and too late, while populations and cities steadily grew in size, and the cry grew increasingly loud for more food, more freedom, more opportunity, more and better education, improved health, more space, and better houses in which to live.

In Puerto Rico the cry for improvement, muted for centuries, at last rose clearly and unmistakably in the form of the revolutionary election of 1940. Because the United States—harassed by the world depression, the rise of communism, and the outbreak of World War II—heeded that cry and granted the island's colonial subjects the rights and powers to help themselves, with the direct help of the United States if they wished, the Commonwealth is now in a position to help the United States carry out its epoch-making program of hemispheral unity. The Kennedy administration is the first in Washington to recognize Puerto Rico's modern transformation as something more than a series of programs and projects. It is the first officially to regard that transformation as a great human experience, resulting from and contributing to powerful modern historical trends and therefore important to all the world and especially to Latin America.

CHANGES IN THE UNITED STATES

The lesson which the present administration wishes to dramatize through Puerto Rico is not merely that the island has been transformed in recent decades, but that the United States has also been transformed and is being further transformed at an accelerating pace. Not only the United States government, but also much of North American capital, as well as a slowly growing section of the United States public, realize that the situation of a prosperous United States, living side by side with a stricken, exploited Latin America disturbed by the revolutionary clamor of its inchoate masses, cannot continue much longer. The lessons of World War II, when the need for hemispheric self-sufficiency in strategic raw materials was as dramatically evident as was that for strong and pro-

ductive, rather than weak and socially restless allies, contributed to
that dawning realization. So did the rise of communism and the
distressing modern example of Cuba's revolutionary directions. Far
more powerful, however, was the modern world's dawning convic-
tion that Lincoln's statement to the effect that the nation could not
survive half slave and half free must now be expanded to read that
the world of democratic capitalism can no longer survive half free
and half feudal or colonial.

Puerto Rico, which was never even remotely threatened by communism and which produced no strategic raw materials except the
sugar which many other societies were struggling so hard to produce and sell that it had to be put on a quota, is an outstanding example of the results of that ideological revolution within capitalism
itself. Meanwhile it is no wonder that the use of Puerto Rico for
implementing the Alliance for Progress is today, as stated in Chapter I, being attacked so bitterly from both the far left and the far
right, on the ground that the island is still a stricken, exploited colony. The communists at the left, and the feudal landlords on the
right, have equally to lose from a successful Alliance for Progress
and must therefore remain unflinching and unanimous in their
condemnation of the United States as a heartless, imperialistic ex-
ploiter, adamant in its evil designs on Latin America.

THE ANSWER TO COMMUNISM

But while the verbal war rages, all the Latin American societies,
aided by the United States and at times inspired by Puerto Rico,
though often impeded by their own upper classes, are planning
their own programs for social, economic, and political salvation.
Puerto Rico has in the past been called, by a few enthusiastic observers, "America's answer to communism." Today, in reply to
Fidel Castro and all that he stands for, a Washington administration
is openly calling it precisely that, not only in its hemispheric affairs
but also, to a lesser degree, in its worldwide struggle to gain the
strong friends and allies who, in the final analysis, constitute the
most powerful weapon imaginable in the fearful modern world
struggle.

Bibliography

Diffie, Bailey and Justine, *Porto Rico, A Broken Pledge,* Vanguard, 1931.

Friedrich, Carl J., *Puerto Rico, Middle Road to Freedom,* Rinehart, 1959.

Hanson, Earl Parker, *Transformation, the Story of Modern Puerto Rico,* Simon and Schuster, 1955. *Puerto Rico, Land of Wonders,* Alfred A. Knopf, 1960.

Jones, Clarence, and Picó, Rafael, *Symposium on the Geography of Puerto Rico,* University of Puerto Rico Press, 1955.

Koenig, Nathan, *A Comprehensive Agriculture Program for Puerto Rico,* United States Department of Agriculture, in cooperation with the Commonwealth of Puerto Rico.

Morales Carrión, Arturo, *Puerto Rico and the Non-Hispanic Caribbean,* University of Puerto Rico Press, 1952.

Pagán, Bolívar, *Historia de los Partidos Políticos Puertorriqueños,* Librería Campos, 1959.

Perloff, Harvey, *Puerto Rico's Economic Future,* The University of Chicago Press, 1950.

Picó, Rafael, *The Geographic Regions of Puerto Rico,* University of Puerto Rico Press, 1950. *Geografía de Puerto Rico,* University of Puerto Rico Press, 1954.

Tugwell, Rexford, *The Stricken Land,* Doubleday, 1946.

Index